Other Books by David W. Anderson

Toward a Theology of Special Education: Integrating Faith and Practice, WestBow Press, 2012. (Also translated and published in Korean.)

Reaching Out and Bringing In: Ministry to and with Persons with Disabilities, WestBow Press, 2013. (Also translated and published in Russian and Korean.)

Forty Days: Finding Refuge in the Ark from the Storms of Disability. WestBow Press, 2018. (Also translated and published in Russian.)

READING PAUL
THROUGH THE EYES
OF DISABILITY

Practical Theological Implications for Inclusive Ministry

DAVID W. ANDERSON

WESTBOW
PRESS®
A DIVISION OF THOMAS NELSON
& ZONDERVAN

WestBow Press books may be ordered through booksellers or by contacting:

WestBow Press
A Division of Thomas Nelson & Zondervan
1663 Liberty Drive
Bloomington, IN 47403
www.westbowpress.com
844-714-3454

ISBN: 978-1-6642-4211-1 (sc)
ISBN: 978-1-6642-4213-5 (hc)
ISBN: 978-1-6642-4212-8 (e)

Library of Congress Control Number: 2021915871

Print information available on the last page.

WestBow Press rev. date: 08/16/2021

ENDORSEMENTS

After reading the manuscript, I thought, "Why is he preaching to the choir?" I know this stuff. I believe this stuff. I practice this stuff (as best as I can, though I know I fail to live up to what David encourages in this book far too often). And I preach this stuff. Then I shared my thoughts with a few of my friends whose ministry focus is different than mine. One friend focuses his life on prison ministry. He reads and interprets Scripture based on passages through the lens of God's heart for folks in jail. Another friend has dedicated her life to assisting women in crisis pregnancy situations. And other whose life is dedicated to helping Christians get out of debt and begin to handle their money "God's way."

You guessed it. Each person reads and interprets Scripture based on passages that "prove their point." And each of them brings important perspectives that we, as the body of Christ, need to hear. In this book, David does something a bit different. Rather than picking verses in (or out) of context here and there, attempting to lead us to a pre-drawn conclusion, he takes us through 1 and 2 Corinthians as if we, the reader, are sitting in a wheelchair listening to the apostle read to us from his audio-book. David guides us through the timeless truths of Scripture and encourages us to read them with a different pair of glasses – ones informed by disability. And in doing so, we begin to see truths that we might never have seen before.

I encourage you to read this book. And then I challenge you to read the Bible in a whole new way. Perhaps the way God intended us to read it: "focused on the eternal and all-powerful God from the perspective of our own weakness."

Steve Boles, Executive Director, Mission to Ukraine

God's Word does not speak directly to the human dilemma surrounding disability, but humans wrestle with these things all of the time. Perhaps God does not address these issues because his main concern is with the eternal portion of humankind, what we call the "heart." As we wrestle with issues of disability, our task is to see and treat people as the Creator does: people made in His image. David Anderson emphasizes this truth in examining that truth within the writing of the Apostle Paul. His book illuminates what the Lord said to the prophet Samuel: "for God sees not as man sees, for man looks at the outward appearance, but the Lord looks at the heart" (1 Samuel 6:7). "Reading Paul through the Eyes of Disability" reminds us that God's view is different than ours. While we look at the external, God focuses on a person's eternal, invisible (to us) character. God's desire is for repentance and faith to salvation for everyone.

Dana Croxton, Founder of Enable Ministries – Training the Body of Christ for In-home Care of the Ill, Injured and Disabled as Evangelism.

David and Florence Anderson are not only friends and coworkers in ministry, especially ministry to persons living with disabilities, but most importantly, they have a heart for the needy and work to help the church of the Lord Jesus Christ be aware of this need that it has for long ignored.

Reading Paul through the eyes of disability is a masterpiece that clearly brings out the heart of God for people who are weak and vulnerable, as explained in Paul's epistles to the Corinthians. By careful and insightful research by the author, David clearly shows that God's heart goes out to the disabled.

His passion and love for persons living with disabilities serve as our guide as we follow Jesus Christ's heart in serving the disabled. Disability ministry should be given priority in Church.

Bishop Hudson Bande, B.A. in Bible and Theology. The King's Ambassadors Christian Ministries International, Nairobi, Kenya

CONTENTS

THEMES

FOREWORD

This book is primarily for the benefit of the local church. It will help the church's leaders to be grounded in a biblical understanding of God's heart for the disabled. Its ultimate goal, however, is not simply to convince us of this truth, but for the church to welcome these persons and their families as equals and as important to the church's fellowship and service.

The author, Dr. David Anderson, has the training and experience to address this topic. He taught special education for a number of years at Bethel University and is the author of several other books on this topic. Dr. Anderson has also taught on ministry to the disabled in many countries, including Haiti, Ukraine, Kenya, and Serbia. But, unlike his other books, which tended to be more theological and academic, *Reading Paul through the Eyes of Disability* is more concerned to encourage application.

Dr. Anderson here provides valuable insights into the biblical text of especially 1 and 2 Corinthians with immediate application regarding how the church views and responds to the disabled. A few sample quotations from the book will illustrate this point:

> "Disability is a reminder that we live in a damaged, sin-filled world, that the present world is itself disabled."

> "When God looks at a person who is disabled, he does not see a person of limited value but someone through whom he can display his greatness."

> "It is those without a disability, including Christians and church leaders, who seem to question God's ability to work in and through people who are disabled."

> "We recognize and respect the limitations resulting from physical or intellectual disability, but we understand that the *person* is not 'a disability.' We do not judge them as the world does: they are

not 'poor unfortunates' to be cast aside, kept out of sight, or terminated through abortion or denial of medical care."

"Having Christ at our side does not necessitate the removal of a disability. Instead, we should seek God's wisdom and 'cure' for our attitude and allow him to use believers in their weakness or disability for his glory. It is not about us; it is about him."

"A disability does not prevent a Christian from demonstrating joy and contentment nor limit the ability to bring blessing to others. Even a severe physical impairment and inability to speak do not affect the ability to express love and peace to others."

"…arranging the room for worship, handing out worship folders, and cleaning up afterward are things which can be done even by someone who is intellectually challenged – quite possibly done more meticulously and joyfully than able-bodied folks, and with no expectation of earthly (financial) reward."

"Asking a person who is disabled to pray, serve, or read scripture honors both them and the God we serve."

The main part of the book includes twenty readings based on selected passages from First and Second Corinthians. Each reading averages about 6 or 7 pages in length, which I found helpful to read as daily devotionals. You may be helped by doing something similar. But regardless of your reading practice, over time, the variety of readings will no doubt challenge you toward appropriate loving action in serving a segment of the population, the disabled, which the world and the church have often overlooked.

It is my prayer that this book will lead to practical change and appropriate action.

Dr. Richard C. Schoenert
Pastor Emeritus, Calvary Church, Roseville, MN
Missionary, One Challenge International
Adjunct Professor at Kremenchuk Evangelical Seminary (Ukraine)
Chair of the Board of Directors of READ Ministries, Saint Cloud, MN
Associate Staff Member, VitalChurch Ministry

INTRODUCTION

After graduating from college with a degree in Bible, thoughts about seminary were put on hold while I sought God's direction for further studies, possibly in the field of education, and enrolled in evening classes at Temple University to explore this route. Through a series of what, at the time, seemed like random occurrences, God directed me into a lifetime career focusing on special education and disability-related issues. My interest in this began when a gentleman from the business office shared a copy of *Psychology Today,* saying, "I thought you might be interested in this." His visit was a God-arranged encounter since it is doubtful that he knew I had enrolled in a course in educational psychology. As I began to leaf through the magazine during my lunch break, an article dealing with neurochemistry and Down syndrome caught my attention. Though I understood little of the article's content, I have a vivid recollection of the accompanying photograph of a six-year-old girl who had Down syndrome. I thought she was one of the most beautiful children I had ever seen. God used that photograph to plant an interest in special education in my heart and mind.

Shortly after beginning my first course, an introduction to exceptionalities, I sensed something essentially "Christian" about working with children and adults with a disability. Earning advanced degrees in special education and practical theology, and ongoing experience with individuals and families affected by disability, allowed that conviction to grow. I find it challenging to read almost any passage in the Bible without seeing some connection with or application to ministry to and with persons and families affected by disability. Without a personal connection with disability, seminarians and church leaders rarely recognize this relationship. The inability of a nondisabled person to see how the Bible relates to disability and the difficulties faced by those who deal with disability daily is understandable, but reveals a significant omission in terms of evangelism and pastoral care. Even persons with a disabling condition, congenital or acquired through accident, illness, or aging, often miss this connection.

The focus of this book

In *Reaching out and bringing in: Ministry to and with persons with disabilities* (Anderson, 2013), my focus was more academic, looking at theological themes and practical aspects of ministry to and with people and families dealing with a disability. The present book is intended to help the church gain a biblical approach to disability and welcome these individuals and families as equal and vital members of the fellowship. Emphasis is on the practical, everyday implications of theology to life experiences and relationships within the church, following Browning's (1981) thought that a practical theology of care defines how the church should relate in a helping way to individuals and groups in the church and in the world. Practical theology pertains to what our actions say to others and the credibility of our Christian witness, focusing on things like biblical justice, compassion, hospitality, and Christlike character.

Paul, of course, is not directly teaching about disability. But much of his writing bears on how Christians, and the church as a whole, should relate to others, nondisabled or disabled, with acceptance, love, humility, patience, and equality. The primary focus is on Paul's epistles to the church at Corinth, though other passages from the Old and New Testaments are addressed when appropriate. Though not a commentary in the traditional sense, this book seeks to help Christians read Paul through the eyes of disability to understand the experience of individuals and families affected by disability and how the church often fails to minister to their spiritual needs. I will highlight the applications and implications of Paul's writing related to disability ministry and relationships with individuals and families facing issues of disability. I hope to remove a veil, as it were, that blinds nondisabled persons to the beauty of those who are disabled and need Christ as much as nondisabled people, and to understand that God loves and can use people just the way they are, even if that includes being disabled. Attention will be drawn to issues addressed by Paul in 1 and 2 Corinthians that parallel conditions faced by those with disabilities, such as oneness in diversity, Godly foolishness versus human wisdom, weakness, God-centered relationships, spiritual gifting, and comfort, love, and reconciliation, among others. Together, these focus on a Christian worldview and changes in heart and spirit.

I write in the same spirit as Yong (2011), who sought to help readers rethink disability, recognizing that the Bible has often been read in a way that marginalizes people with a disability. The problem, wrote Yong, centers on the fact that nondisabled people unconsciously assume their experience to be the "norm," concluding that a person with a disability is, therefore, "not-normal." The result is a *normate bias* towards people who are disabled which functions at a subconscious level. Never questioned or examined, the normate bias shapes how people look at their experience and the assumptions, often erroneous, made about the experience of someone with a physical or intellectual impairment. Encountering someone with an obvious disability often creates emotional disequilibrium because of fear of becoming disabled, leading to avoidance of persons with a significant disability. Looking at scripture through a lens of disability will challenge those who relegate people with a disability to the margins of society and the Kingdom, and at the same time, empower believers who are disabled. Greater awareness can help churches avoid common expressions which unwittingly exclude a disabled person, such as asking people to stand for prayer or the reading of God's Word without the proviso "if you are able" (although even this may draw unnecessary attention to the person), or saying "as you can clearly see" when there could be someone with a visual impairment in the congregation. While such expressions are not intended to push persons aside, leaders must be aware of the words and phrases they use without thinking.

The negative effect of the normate worldview

The normate worldview colors the way people who have a disability are viewed and often excluded. Because disability is alien to their experience, some nondisabled persons may feel uncomfortable being around a person who has a disability, especially if the disability is severe. They may fear that person or may experience self-oriented anxiety, imagining how their life would be different if they became disabled. Parents sometimes pull their children away from someone who is severely disabled, sending an unspoken message that such people are to be avoided, potentially developing in the child a generalized fear of people who are disabled which, should that child become disabled through illness or accident, could create a barrier to self-acceptance or even concern about whether the parent still loves the child.

People with a disability, if admitted to the church, may still be pushed aside, physically, emotionally, or spiritually, allowing nondisabled persons to maintain the false belief that they have control over events in their life. The overt rejection or covert avoidance of individuals and families dealing with a disability "defines" them as unacceptable – a feeling not lost to those with a disability, but surely not the way God sees them.

Many Christians believe God chooses to reveal himself only through extraordinary displays of supernatural power, thus drawing attention to God's awesomeness (Frost, 2000). God's speaking to Moses from the burning bush that was not consumed (Exodus 3), God's parting the waters to enable Israel to cross over on the dry ground (Exodus 14), and the many miracles performed by Jesus are examples of God's revealing himself through the extraordinary and unexpected. Focusing only on these examples of God's self-revelation causes us to miss seeing God acting in and through "ordinary" people, including ordinary people who have a disability. Some churches may conclude that God cannot work in and through someone who is disabled and insist that God must miraculously remove what, to them, is a handicapping condition (reflecting their discomfort regarding disability).

Do we then limit God's ability to minister to and through people with certain types and degrees of disability? Frost (2000) urged being attentive to how God often reveals himself in unusual ways and through unexpected people. He reasons that society (and we can add, the church) is in bad shape when people are objectified and reduced to what they can do or offer us, adding that "You love God as much, and no more, than the person you love the least" (p. 154). What does that say to Christians or churches which neglect or reject people who have a disability? Our spiritual eyes must remain open to see God's grace and beauty revealed in ordinary people and ordinary experiences, including the experience of severe physical or intellectual impairment. To accede to culture's (or churches') devaluation of people who are disabled is to limit God's ability to reveal grace to us through those individuals.

The Role of the Church

The church must seek to create a community where people who are not alike can live and work together to present a visible expression of God's love for all humanity. Concern for social justice toward and inclusion of persons with a disability affirms the church to be a reconciled and reconciling community. The gospel is for persons of any physical, mental, and psychological circumstances, not simply those who conform to the world's norms (Tiffany & Ringe, 1996).

Hauerwas (2004) wrote, "the most stringent power we have over another is not physical coercion but the ability to have the other accept our definition of them" (p. 37). This negative power principle often shows in the Christian church, where nondisabled persons have the "power" to impose their definition on people with disabilities. But their definition is usually based on a lack of accurate knowledge of disability or the specific individual, false and unjustified assumptions, and false theology. Nonetheless, people with disabilities are expected to accept and adapt to the norms of the powerful. As a result, the individual or family dealing with disability is not entirely welcomed as *belonging* to the body. Being considered less important, if not completely excluded, persons with a disability may be pushed to the back row of the worship center to limit their visible presence, thereby reinforcing the false notion that being disabled is not acceptable to the church or to God. How the church treats people with disabilities reflects the kind of God we follow, and can negatively impact how they view both Christianity and God. Pushing aside or not allowing persons with a disability to be a part of the Church gives the impression that God's grace, love, and salvation are only for people who are nondisabled.

God does not evaluate people based on what they can contribute to the church (or the world); God accepts all persons through Christ. The Church finds its true identity when it fully integrates marginalized people: the diseased and disabled, widows and orphans, people of different cultures or ethnicity, and others who are rejected or oppressed by the majority culture. God's desire for the Church is that it be inclusive and communally-oriented, characterized by reconciliation and embrace, and demonstrating concern "for the well-being of the neighbor and radical hospitality to the stranger" (Johnson, 1989, p. 47). Jesus's parable of the good Samaritan (Luke 10:29-37) teaches that "neighbor" includes people *unlike* us. As a covenant community, the Church is not homogeneous. It consists of a variety of people, including the poor, disabled, illiterate, and aged – people represented in Jesus's parable of the great banquet (Luke 14).

Why focus on disability?

When disability comes into a person's or a family's life, by genetic cause or through accident or illness, a new world is entered – not by choice, but by necessity. Whether or not the person is a believer, questions arise related to God's character, wisdom, love, and goodness: Why has God allowed this? Is God angry with me? Am I being punished by God for something I have done or not done?

No one asks to become disabled or to give birth to a child with a disabling condition, and no one is emotionally prepared when disability enters their life. Most people go through life with an unconscious expectation that disability only happens to other people. Thus, the entrance of disability into a person's or family's life is a critical time for the Church to step forward. Church leaders (pastors, elders, deacons, Sunday school teachers, youth workers, members of the choir, or missionaries) who have not considered disability from a biblical perspective cannot respond biblically to questions about God's involvement in disability. They may be unsure of how they and the Church can minister to the individual and family.

An appropriate response requires more than presenting a vague theological discussion; always, theology needs to have a practical application. The spiritual struggles and feelings of persons faced with disability are real and often lead to spiritual crisis. Seminary-trained persons who respond in such a situation with a scholarly discussion of the problem of evil and suffering fail to recognize the personal nature of the question. Approaching the question academically, even though strong theological points can be raised, will be unhelpful to the family for whom the issue is deeply emotional and spiritual. Christian theology is life-oriented and has ethical implications for how we view ourselves and how we view individuals and families confronted with disability. Church leaders who have not reflected theologically on issues of disability may respond with unhelpful biblical platitudes. Giesbrecht (1988) provided an apt illustration. As a young child, her son, Jeremy, was diagnosed as having a neurological disorder (autism). During childhood, Jeremy was severely burned. Giesbrecht related how several church friends offered suggestions as to why this happened to her son, which perhaps made them feel comfortable, but brought no comfort to his parents and cannot be supported by scripture. Their "counseling" included the notion that God allowed Jeremy's suffering to promote spiritual growth in his parents, to make their values more Christ-like, to help others believe in God, or to bring glory to God (Giesbrecht, 1988, p. 156). Perhaps the most unhelpful (and most outlandish) idea was that God was burning the autism out of Jeremy (p. 103).

As Christians, we recognize that people are more than their biological make-up or mental acuity: "We are children of God, and individually we are members together in the body of Christ" (Webb-Mitchell, 2008, p. xv). All people, disabled and nondisabled, are created as God's image (Genesis 1:26–27), individually designed by God (Psalm 139), and called to be children of God (John 1:12–13). Being created as God's image is our primary identity, not being able-bodied or disabled. People cannot be reduced to their "condition," nor understood simply as disabled persons. Biblical teaching must be the starting point for ministry to and with persons and families dealing with disability. Jesus welcomed all who came to him, but he did not always wait for them to approach him. At times, Jesus seemed to go out of his way to reach people – such as Zacchaeus (Luke 19) or the woman of Samaria (John 4).

Since all believers belong to a community of faith, the actions or attitudes of one person affect the community as a whole (Guthrie, 1981). The same is true when disability enters the picture: the whole family and the whole church are impacted. If the Church rejects or ignores individuals or families struggling with disabilities, what message do they receive from the Church? The primary element of Christian ethics is love for God and love for one's neighbor. Love should transcend and transform human relationships, giving evidence of the Holy Spirit's work in the life of a believer. How we interact with individuals and families affected by disability will show either love or its absence. Do we regard them as equals, as children of God? Do we treat them as "lesser than" able-bodied persons? Are they *welcomed* into fellowship or merely tolerated? Are they respected as individuals? Are they given opportunities to serve in Church?

Some may question whether a child or adult with a severe intellectual or physical disability can benefit from attending a worship service. But this question reflects wrong thinking or inadequate theology. We worship God to *give,* not to receive. Worship is not merely a cognitive act; it is a spiritual act. Questioning whether a person with a severe intellectual impairment can understand and respond to the gospel message is to forget the principle which Jesus explained to his disciples when the rich young man walked away saddened (Matthew 19:22). Expecting that a wealthy person is "approved" by God, they asked, "who then can be saved?" In response, Jesus said, with man, it is impossible, but with God, *all* things are possible (Matthew 19:26). God saves, not our intellectual or physical ability. Even a person with an intellectual disability, because he or she is a human person, can be engaged by rituals like worship, perhaps even to a deeper level than nondisabled persons whose attention may wander to what someone is wearing or what songs are being sung.

Lawrence (2010) suggested that our knowledge of God draws from knowing and observing the world around us (p. 104). People gain some understanding of God even in the context of disability, often from the way they are treated by Christians who are able-bodied, such as understanding that God is a God of love who cared for humankind deeply enough that he sent his Son to die for us. Disability, our own or that of a loved one, is not a detriment to learning about God and grace, but what is learned depends on our response to disability and the person with the disability.

Because all human beings are made in the image of God, there is an "equality of right to life that is not conditioned on ability, capacity, or usefulness" (Lawrence, 2010, p. 106). The church can help individuals with a disability discover how they can bring glory to God and serve him even though disabled. Church leaders often face problems and questions that require searching God's Word for answers, guidance, and wisdom. But it is not abstract theological ideas that give the answers to intensely practical questions, especially when disability is the focus. Thinking theologically about disability includes seeking to understand the "place" and purpose of disability in general and how (and why) to minister with persons who have a disabling condition. This involves recognizing that God has designed and gifted each person, and God can bring glory to himself despite a person's being disabled. Church leaders must be prepared to assist families and individuals affected by disability navigate these profoundly theological questions.

Many churches are slow to respond to families affected by disability, claiming they cannot accommodate them, usually without asking what, if any, accommodations are needed. Asking how they can accommodate the individual or family shows both a welcoming attitude and a willingness to be of service. But to ask how the Church can assist, serve, and include them in its fellowship is rarely the response the individual or family receives. Churches often naively assume the family must change, or the person with a disability must be "fixed" before being welcomed in the Church. Some may incorrectly think the individual or family has insufficient faith to be cured, thereby conveying that they are not welcome without a cure. Other churches claim they cannot meet the family's needs because they lack special training or qualification to serve persons who have a disability. Such excuses reveal the failure to recognize that God can use anyone for his purposes, even someone with a severe or profound disability. Or the excuses simply convey that the church does not want to be bothered.

Soila is a young woman in Kenya with whose family I have ministered. Though Soila has a significant cognitive impairment, perhaps with a hint of autism, her spiritual gift is her ability to draw others more deeply into worship. When the worship music starts, she immediately moves to the front and begins to "dance," swaying awkwardly and spinning, with a beautiful smile and her hands pointing toward heaven. Though unable to speak and somewhat resistant to physical contact from people she does not know, Soila's actions touch people's hearts and, no doubt, bring a smile to God's face as well.

We must never assume that God cannot work in and through a person with a disability to reveal something about himself through that person. God is greater than and sovereign over disability. Our interactions with persons with disabilities and our involvement in their lives can broaden not only their understanding of God, faith, and spirituality but ours as well.

WHY PAUL? WHY CORINTHIANS?

Can a theology of disability be built from Paul's epistles? Not exactly. But as author Jeff McNair (2016) observed, "We may not need a 'disability theology' but we definitely need a theology awakened by disability" (p. 76). Though there will always be a degree of mystery because God's understanding is far beyond ours, continued attention to all of God's revelation is necessary to arrive at a comprehensive biblical view of disability. Nevertheless, Paul has much to say that can help us gain a proper perspective on the "place" of disability and weakness in a Christian's life and how the church can effectively and respectfully minister to and with families and individuals whose lives are impacted by disability.

Hughes (2008) asked, "If it is true that God is at work in every detail of our lives, how do we begin to recognize God's action and our reaction?" (p. 78). Looking at Jesus's actions in the gospels provides a glimpse of what we are to be in Christ, and looking at Paul's teaching through the lens of disability helps us learn how to model Jesus's life and ministry with and among people who are disabled. Jesus's example and Paul's teaching clearly show that our ministry's central element must be compassion. But do Christians and Christian churches display compassion toward individuals and families whose lives are affected by disability? How is that compassion to be shown, and what evidence is there that such compassion is lacking?

Paul is the author of nearly half the New Testament and wrote much about living the Christian life. Though he was not writing specifically on disability issues, Paul's teachings are relevant to how people with a disability are seen and how we as Christians are to relate to them as people of worth and people whom God loves. Based on passages such as 2 Corinthians 12:7–10, Galatians 4:13–15, and Galatians 6:11, Yong (2011) wondered whether Paul might have been the first theologian with a disability.

In Acts 4:9, we read of a man being cured of his physical disability and joining Peter and John in praising God for his cure. However, we must not assume the most urgent need is for a physical cure, nor should we conclude that a person needs to be made physically or mentally "whole" through a miracle or medical procedure to become an active participant in the church's life. God can use a person in his or her disabled state to bring glory to himself, perhaps even more so *because* of that person's apparent "weakness." The idea that disability must be removed speaks more about our discomfort and fear of how our lives would be altered if we became disabled than of concern for the individual.

Rather than something that must be removed, disability can become a tool or vehicle by which God brings blessing to people and glory to himself, not by eliminating the disability but through healing the person's spirit, giving testimony to God's grace and provision (cf. Anderson, 2013). Barnett (1988) asserted that the influence of God's power on man is not related to man's supposed strength but to man's fundamental weakness. This theological insight is evident throughout Paul's writing (especially in 2 Corinthians).

We can draw a parallel between the Corinthian church's problems or attitudes and similar attitudes in today's churches surrounding disability. For nondisabled persons, issues include prejudicial attitudes stemming from ignorance about and unfamiliarity with disability, or deceptive assumptions about disability (such as the notion that unconfessed sin caused the disability or that a person's lack of faith prevents being cured), and the unfounded idea that persons with a disability are of little value because they have nothing to "give" to the Church. For persons with a disability, issues of fear, despair, and loneliness also need to be dispelled, which the Church is eminently capable of doing. Looking at Paul's teaching through the lens of disability can reveal and correct wrong heart attitudes and lead to people dealing with disability being blessed, encouraged, and empowered to serve the Lord.

In 2 Corinthians 10:5, Paul wrote, "We demolish arguments and every pretension that sets itself up against the knowledge of God, and we take captive every thought to make it obedient to Christ." Concerning persons with disabilities, this includes thoughts about *who* they are and *why* they are. The Bible teaches that all people are created in (or as) the image of God. "*All* people" does not refer only to nondisabled persons but also includes people born with a disability or who have become disabled through accident, illness, or aging. How we regard and treat people with a disability must be in concert with the biblical truth of being in God's image. Anything less than respect, love, and compassion is an insult to God's claim to be Creator and Lord of all. Since all human life is set apart for the glory of God, Christians have a moral obligation to preserve, promote, and bring healing (not curing) to all human life, acting as agents of God's mercy. A person's right to life is not conditioned on their ability, capacity, or usefulness (Lawrence, 2010). People are not defined by their behavior or ability to think, move, see, or hear. What being created in (or as) the image of God means is beyond the scope of this book, but Reynolds (2008) provided a broad view that is instructive for our consideration.

> (To) be created in the image of God means to be created for contributing to the world, open toward the call to love others. Three dimensions are implied: creativity with others, relation to others, and availability to others. The point to be stressed is that *all people* can be contributors, representing a range of both gifts and limitations. *Disability is not an incomplete humanity in this regard* (p. 177; emphasis added).

Paul founded the church in Corinth during his second missionary journey. He probably remained in Corinth for about eighteen months (cf. Acts 18:1–18) to establish a firm foundation before moving on. Both epistles to the Corinthians deal with similar issues and were written out of love for the people of Corinth and in response to learning of problems in the church, which had created internal strife and division. He reminded them that they were God's people and that actions and attitudes matter. The intent of his teaching was corrective and designed to deepen their understanding of proper church behavior and how to live for Christ in a corrupt society.

Themes within the two epistles that relate to the church's approach to disability include unity and diversity, human foolishness and Godly wisdom, and grace and reconciliation. 1 Corinthians 1–11 reveals a pastor's heart as Paul responds to the matters requiring correction. Chapters 12–16 continue Paul's instruction but are more directly theological (yet practical) regarding the church and living together as believers.

2 Corinthians, written shortly after the first epistle while Paul was in Macedonia (2 Corinthians 7:5, 8:1), was to affirm his ministry and authority as an apostle, disprove false teachers in Corinth, and encourage the believers in their obedience. Second Corinthians seems to present a more impassioned appeal out of sincere concern that they are not drawn astray by false teaching in the church. He reminded them that he is an ambassador for Christ, while reluctantly speaking of his personal weakness (2 Corinthians 12), and encouraged them to "fix" the problems in the church so that when he revisited Corinth, he would be able to devote his time to building them up rather than disciplining them.

Paul's teaching in the two epistles to Corinth is directly informative to ministry to and with individuals and families who deal with issues accompanying disability, particularly his stress on unity and mutual love. Paul was not so much underscoring the need for ministry to individuals and families who deal with disability but with the need for the church to develop relationships with them, fully incorporating all believers in the family of Christ. McNair's comment is to the point: "If my understanding of who God is results in me NOT loving all of his human creation then I don't understand who God is" (2016, p. 76; emphasis in original). It is hoped that this book will encourage full acceptance of people with disabilities into the body of Christ and a deeper understanding of the heart of the God we serve.

THEMES

CALLED TO UNITY

Paul, called by the will of God to be an apostle of Christ Jesus, and our brother Sosthenes, to the church of God that is in Corinth, to those sanctified in Christ Jesus, called to be saints together with all those who in every place call upon the name of our Lord Jesus Christ, both their Lord and ours: Grace to you and peace from God our Father and the Lord Jesus Christ. I give thanks to my God always for you because of the grace of God that was given you in Christ Jesus, that in every way you were enriched in him in all speech and all knowledge–even as the testimony about Christ was confirmed among you–so that you are not lacking in any gift, as you wait for the revealing of our Lord Jesus Christ, who will sustain you to the end, guiltless in the day of our Lord Jesus Christ. God is faithful, by whom you were called into the fellowship of his Son, Jesus Christ our Lord. I appeal to you, brothers, by the name of our Lord Jesus Christ, that all of you agree, and that there be no divisions among you, but that you be united in the same mind and the same judgment. For it has been reported to me by Chloe's people that there is quarreling among you, my brothers. What I mean is that each one of you says "I follow Paul," or "I follow Apollos," or "I follow Cephas," or "I follow Christ." Is Christ divided? Was Paul crucified for you? Or were you baptized in the name of Paul? thank God that I baptized none of you except Crispus and Gaius, so that no one may say that you were baptized in my name ... For Christ did not send me to baptize but to preach the gospel, and not with words of eloquent wisdom, lest the cross of Christ be emptied of its power.

1 Corinthians 1:1–14, 17

Paul opens 1 Corinthians with his customary greeting, identifying himself as an apostle of Jesus Christ by the will of God. He writes with authority but acknowledges that apostleship was not something he sought for himself; it is a role to which God appointed him. Though Paul established the Church in Corinth, it is not his church, but God's. The Greek word translated "church" (*ekklesia*) refers to people God has called out from the world into fellowship with himself and with one another. This includes all people everywhere who call on the name of the Lord Jesus – *all* people, without regard to ethnicity, nationality, gender, age, or physical and mental ability. God's calling us into fellowship with himself indicates that we have done nothing to earn God's favor, nor do we have characteristics or abilities which God needs. It is solely by God's doing that we are made saints and become united to the Lord and interconnected with one another.

This is important because not including individuals and families affected by disability suggests that people disabled from birth or from an accident or illness are less important or of lesser worth and have nothing to contribute to the church. Even if unconsciously made, evidence of this assumption is the absence of an intentional ministry to and with persons and families dealing with disability and the small number of disabled persons among the fellowship of believers. Nondisabled people may consider themselves more valuable to the gospel, suggesting a sense of superiority and perhaps the thought that God is blessed to have them as part of the church. Paul rehearses for his readers the essential truth of the gospel: God's grace and peace are given to believers through Christ, leading to their spiritual enrichment and gifting from God, and assuring them that God, because he is faithful, will keep them strong until the day of the Lord.

The Christian's call carries an ethical demand for holy living, making our vocation, as "those who have been made saints by God to become in daily obedience what [we] are in Christ Jesus" (Wilson, 1971, p. 15). Being called into fellowship with Jesus Christ implies that believers are also called into fellowship with one another, be they able-bodied or disabled. But unity was not a characteristic displayed in the Corinthian church. In 1:10, Paul raised the problem of divisions and practices in the church that led to disunity: lack of agreement with one another, lawsuits, and immoral activity. He urged the Corinthian believers to agree with one another, to be perfectly united in mind and thought – "mind" not referring to the intellect but to a heart and spirit of oneness in Christ. Paul focused extensively on the wisdom of the Spirit in contrast to the foolishness of the people. The Corinthians, being a product of Greek culture, were influenced by Greek ideas of wisdom. This, Paul explained, is why he did not present the gospel with lofty words but with the power of the Holy Spirit (2:1–4). In a somewhat parallel manner, many church members today seem influenced by the "wisdom" of the world, particularly (in our focus) on how disability is understood and how people with disabilities are excluded or unwelcome rather than approached as accepted.

Paul said believers do not lack any spiritual gift as they wait for the Lord to be revealed (1:17). Some question whether this gifting applies to a believer who is disabled, especially if the disability is severe. But is God limited regarding who can receive spiritual gifts? Asking whether a person with a disability can have a spiritual gift reveals ignorance about disability, seemingly lumping all types and degrees of disability together, and ignorance about God's gifting. The question suggests that disability makes a person unworthy or incapable of receiving God's gifts or that disability limits what God can do. At a deeper level, the question raises doubts about God's faithfulness and wisdom in calling people with severe disabilities into fellowship with Jesus (1:9).

Do God's call and gifting apply only to saints who are able-bodied? Is there anyone so disabled that God would not or cannot effectively call that person to himself? Is severe physical or intellectual disability a block to God's effectual call? By ignoring people with a disability, not welcoming them into the fellowship of the body of Christ (or into their hearts), the church takes upon itself a role that is rightly God's. Since we know God does not make mistakes, every believer, whether able-bodied or disabled, is known of God, called by God, graced by God, and gifted by God.

How might the inclusion of individuals and families with disabilities in the faith community transform our understanding of and witness to what Christ has accomplished? How might it alter our understanding of God, God's love, and God's working in the world? How might it change our understanding of humankind and human value? If the Church (or an individual believer) does not welcome someone who has a disability into fellowship, it sends a message that living with a disability is an unacceptable way of being human (or being Christian). Has God said that only nondisabled people are acceptable in the church or in his family?

David W. Anderson

Connor (2012) asserted that churches that do not minister to families dealing with disability leave those families as "spiritual nomads." He wrote:

> Faith communities [should] offer places for people with disabilities to experience social roles, a way to understand themselves beyond pathological self-definitions or medical understandings, and a place to develop social relationships and a sense of belonging and connectedness. This sense of validation and belonging mitigates the hopelessness of loneliness (p. 32).

Able-bodied and disabled persons are unified as equals in the Church, the body of Christ. Thus, there should be no divisions among or separations between people in the church; we all follow Christ, the Head of the Church. Contentiousness toward persons with physical or mental disabilities promotes the idea that nondisabled persons are spiritually superior and that persons with disabilities are inferior, and therefore, not worth the church's concern and remain unwelcome.

In contrast, Paul's words provide a defense for ministry to and with people with a disability, even significant intellectual impairment. Becoming a believer does not necessitate understanding the depth of Paul's theology. People with severe disabilities can have a saving knowledge of Christ, who *is* the gospel (the Good News). They may be thought unable to grasp the intricacies of gospel truth. But the majority of nondisabled Christians may also lack the deep theological understanding which Paul displayed in his epistles. Passing a test of theology is not required for salvation. Someone with intellectual impairment may even *demonstrate* a purer grasp of Christ's love than someone with an advanced degree from a university or seminary.

Nouwen (1997), a trained theologian and pastor, shared his experience of caring for Adam, a young man with severe cerebral palsy. Adam's disability rendered him unable to speak or move, making him entirely dependent on Nouwen's caregiving for grooming, dressing, feeding, and transport to different areas on the campus where he lived. Through his relationship with Adam, Nouwen realized that God reveals himself through even the most disabled persons. Said Nouwen,

Adam was, like all of us, a limited person, more limited than most, and unable to express himself in words. But he was a whole person and a blessed man. In his weakness he became a unique instrument of God's grace. He became a revelation of Christ among us (p. 30).

Building a loving relationship with an individual (or a family) dealing with a disability allows nondisabled persons to recognize that the individual is a human person rather than a pathological condition. The normate view promotes the idea of "ableism," a form of discrimination in attitudes or practices based on the notion that a person with a disability (particularly a severe intellectual or physical disability) is inferior and unworthy of continued life. Ableism lies beneath arguments for abortion. Ableism denies God's love (John 3:13) as well as God's grace (Ephesians 2:5). Ableism interferes with our task of taking the gospel to every people group (Matthew 28:18–20).

GOD'S FOOLISHNESS VS. HUMAN WISDOM

For the word of the cross is folly to those who are perishing, but to those who are being saved is the power of God. For it is written, "I will destroy the wisdom of the wise, and the discernment of the discerning I will thwart." Where is the one who is wise? Where is the scribe? Where is the debater of this age? Has not God made foolish the wisdom of the world? For since, in the wisdom of God, the world did not know God through wisdom, it pleased God through the folly of what we preach to save those who believe. For Jews demand signs and Greeks seek wisdom, but we preach Christ crucified, a stumbling block to Jews and folly to Gentiles, but to those who are called, both Jews and Greeks, Christ the power of God and the wisdom of God. For the foolishness of God is wiser than men, and the weakness of God is stronger than men. For consider your calling, brothers: not many of you were wise according to worldly standards, not many were powerful, not many were of noble birth. But God chose what is foolish in the world to shame the wise; God chose what is weak in the world to shame the strong; God chose what is low and despised in the world, even things that are not, to bring to nothing things that are, so that no human being might boast in the presence of God. And because of him you are in Christ Jesus, who became to us wisdom from God, righteousness and sanctification and redemption, so that, as it is written, "Let the one who boasts, boast in the Lord."

1 Corinthians 1:18–31

Paul wrote out of love for the people at the Corinthian Church, but he had been made aware of divisions among the people that have created internal division and strife: sexually immoral behavior, lawsuits leading believers to go to pagan courts, and eating foods offered to idols. His writing was partly a reprimand, followed by teaching with a corrective intent to deepen their understanding of church order and live for Christ while living in a corrupt society. He also sought to remind and encourage the Corinthians concerning gathering offerings for the poor Christians in Jerusalem.

The "things" Paul placed under the category of foolishness were tied to three groups of people: wise men (philosophers; Greek = *sophos*), scholars (Greek = *grammateus*), and skilled debaters (Greek: *suzetetes*). Paul was not saying these individuals are themselves fools (although if they follow their own ideas, they are, from Paul's perspective, behaving foolishly); it is their ideas that are "foolish" in terms of anything eternal. Phrasing it as he does – asking rhetorical questions, "where is the wise one? ... the scribe? ... the debater?" is Paul's way of saying their lofty ideas have no eternal value.

Paul does not disparage intelligence or having advanced degrees, nor does he downplay the advantages of a good education – at least in terms of our earthly existence. But he highlights the futility of worldly philosophy concerning salvation, or as being necessary to serve God. Being a powerful orator, having a solid reputation as a scholar, or being able to out-argue one's opponents in a debate may be valued by society but will not, in themselves, lead a person to God. Jewish scholars sought "signs," and the Greeks sought "wisdom." Because the death and resurrection of Christ did not fit their worldview, to some in Corinth, it was an absurdity. But from God's (and Paul's) perspective, the characteristics valued by the culture are foolishness and will be destroyed and frustrated by God (cf. Isaiah 29:14).

In 1:19, Paul quoted Isaiah 29:14 to show that God's way of thinking differs from the world's (i.e., human) wisdom. In the context of disability ministry many in the world and in the church, through human understanding, discount people with disabilities, especially if the disability is severe. Some believe that disability results from sin (individual or familial); others take for granted that these individuals will be automatically "adopted" into God's family. Either view has the effect of relieving the church of any responsibility to reach out to such persons. God, however, does not see these individuals as worthless or ministry to them as a waste of time, energy, or resources. Worldly wisdom or intelligence is not infallible and can neither discover nor disprove God.

Beginning at 1:10, Paul described the church at Corinth as being fractured by cliques and quarreling. Divisions among the people led to people identifying themselves as belonging to Paul, Apollos, Cephas, or Christ (1:11–12). Paul's concern about separations and divisions is understandable, but many Christians and churches today quietly mimic similar attitudes by favoring and welcoming able-bodied ("normal" or within specific parameters considered "close-to-normal") people, but separating themselves from, or elevating themselves over people with a significant disability. This separation suggests that disabled persons are less worthy (and therefore less welcomed) than nondisabled, well-educated members. But every member of the Church is part of the body of Christ, and, as Paul will bring out in 1 Corinthians 12, each is essential and necessary for the body to be whole.

As Paul said earlier in chapter 1, Christians are part of God's church because of God's call and work, not ours. No flesh can glory in God's presence (1:25–30). It is not worldly wisdom that brings people to faith in Christ; only the Spirit of God can open spiritually blind eyes. Salvation is entirely from God; human ability or disability matters not. It is not by our physical strength, mental acuity, or personal will that we become part of God's family; it is entirely God's doing. Being able-bodied or able-minded does not advantage a person when it comes to salvation. Salvation is a gift from God, not something we earn.

Paul said God's foolishness is wiser than human wisdom, God's weakness more potent than human strength. To an unbeliever, the facts of the gospel – the death and resurrection of Christ – are foolishness. But what the world considers folly is, in reality, a display of God's power and wisdom. Intellectual, academic, political, or social status do not guarantee God's choice of an individual. God does not seek only people whom the world considers important or admirable. Instead, God reveals himself to humble and open hearts without regard to worldly position or status. Faith does not stand on the wisdom of men but the power of God (1 Corinthians 2:5). Might it be that people with disabilities are more open to God's Spirit because they recognize their physical or intellectual weakness?

Paul explained that worldly wisdom could not understand God's actions (1:18–31). To the world, the preaching of the cross is foolishness; but to believers, it is the power of God. God chose the foolish things to shame the wise, weak things to shame the strong, lowly and despised things to nullify what the world regards as "wise" so that we cannot boast in ourselves

(1:27–29). It is not human strength or intelligence that has brought us to salvation; it is the work of God. Thus, disabled believers are on even ground with nondisabled believers. Some Christians see themselves (and some *churches* see themselves) as better or more important than persons with a significant disability. But God sees no distinction. God saved us by his grace when we, in faith, invited Christ into our lives. We cannot take the credit because salvation is a gift from God. Salvation is not a reward for the good things we have done; we are God's masterpiece, created anew in Christ Jesus, so we can do the good things He planned for us long ago (Ephesians 2:8–10). Wilson (1971) wrote, "Human wisdom may indeed contrive to produce in men an intellectual conviction of the truth of the gospel, but [human wisdom] is powerless to create in them a living faith in God" (p. 40). Advanced degrees and high intelligence may work against a person's coming to Christ because the focus is on "self." Can a person who is severely disabled minister to a nondisabled person? Nouwen's (1997) experience with Adam, mentioned earlier, is a prime example.

Paul wrote much about the contrast between God's wisdom and the foolishness of human ideas, asserting that he did not present the gospel with eloquence or superior wisdom but with the power of God's Holy Spirit (2:1–3). As to the divisions within the church, ideas of superiority over others promotes boastfulness. In 1:31, Paul charged believers to stop bragging about themselves, but instead, "let him who boasts boast in the Lord" (quoting Jeremiah 9:24). Boasting or bragging about self is to be replaced by loving and serving one another (as we will see when considering 1 Corinthians 13).

Bragging is not restricted to boastful words but is also evident in attitudes of superiority which led to certain people being dismissed as unimportant or unnecessary. This includes persons with a significant disability who, because of ignorance about disability or generalized fear or insecurity, remind us that we are all one accident away from becoming disabled but not wanting to think about how that could impact our lives and relationships.

Paul declared that God does not call people to himself because of their wisdom, influence, or noble birth. Instead, God has called the foolish, weak, and lowly so that no one can boast. In the eyes of the world, people with a disability are "foolish, weak, or lowly." But attitudes of

David W. Anderson

pride and self-glorification have no place in a Christian's life. It is not by our choosing that we become part of God's family as if to put God in our debt; it is purely by God's gracious call so that no flesh can glory in God's presence (1:29). Salvation is God's work; our redemption, righteousness, and salvation are through Christ (1:30). People who have a disability may become be models for nondisabled persons because they are keenly aware of their limitations and weaknesses and have no hesitation to "boast" in the Lord, not themselves. Readily acknowledging their limitations and disability, they serve as guides leading nondisabled persons to a fuller understanding of grace. McIntosh (2017) highlighted the irony of God's actions:

> God is thrilled to use the broken, weak, and the forgotten
> to reproach the wise and to disgrace the strong for a bigger
> plan and a greater purpose than we can immediately see.
> God takes great delight in using the unexpected. (p. 62)

God does this to affirm his power so that he receives glory and praise, not man. For Paul, worldly wisdom flows from humankind's rebellion against God and our insistence on making God fit our ideas and desires. "Because God is determined to root out all such human pride, any wisdom is to be rejected which is not based on 'Christ crucified'" (Prior, 1985, p. 40). Some who claim Christ as Lord and Savior acknowledge this but may still act as if they have done God a favor in becoming part of God's church. This often leads them to separate themselves, spiritually and physically, from believers they believe to be beneath them, such as those who have a disability. The fight against human pride is ongoing. The danger of this sinful, prideful attitude is that believers who are disabled may come to view themselves as "lesser than." The church is one body consisting of different parts, but each part, including able-bodied and disabled, is essential.

STRENGTH IN WEAKNESS

And I, when I came to you, brothers, did not come proclaiming to you the testimony of God with lofty speech or wisdom. For I decided to know nothing among you except Jesus Christ and him crucified. And I was with you in weakness and in fear and much trembling, and my speech and my message were not in plausible words of wisdom, but in demonstration of the Spirit and of power, so that your faith might not rest in the wisdom of men but in the power of God. Yet among the mature we do impart wisdom, although it is not a wisdom of this age or of the rulers of this age, who are doomed to pass away. [7]But we impart a secret and hidden wisdom of God, which God decreed before the ages for our glory. ... Now we have received not the spirit of the world, but the Spirit who is from God, that we might understand the things freely given us by God. And we impart this in words not taught by human wisdom but taught by the Spirit, interpreting spiritual truths to those who are spiritual. The natural person does not accept the things of the Spirit of God, for they are folly to him, and he is not able to understand them because they are spiritually discerned. The spiritual person judges all things, but is himself to be judged by no one. For who has understood the mind of the Lord so as to instruct him? But we have the mind of Christ.

1 Corinthians 2:1–6, 12–16

In 1 Corinthians 1, Paul introduced the theme of weakness, declaring that God has chosen weak and foolish things of the world to shame the strong and wise. Paul continued the motif of weakness in this passage from chapter 2, and it will surface again in one form or another in both epistles to the Corinthians and other writings of Paul. Humans tend to consider as heroes people who are strong, powerful, and eloquent speakers. They are our "champions," effectively leading us through our battles, both physical and emotional. But Paul asserts that God does not operate the way the world does. Instead, God uses weakness and foolishness to accomplish his will and his work. Why? So that the glory goes to him, not his creation. Though God works *through* men and women, the power is *his*. God uses the "foolishness" of the gospel to accomplish the redemption of many.

As Paul wrote these words, he was unlikely to be thinking about people who are physically or intellectually disabled. The world's wisdom dismisses these persons as unimportant, but God does not see them that way. Paul's conscious decision was not to follow worldly, natural wisdom but to follow God's way. One does not have to be a scholar to understand the gospel. Faith and understanding of gospel truth are not arrived at through human reasoning, but are things that God's Spirit enables people to apprehend.

Elliot, Kiarie, and Mariamu are three teenagers who, though disabled, demonstrate their love for the Lord and willingness to serve others more readily than many Christians who are not disabled. Elliot has cerebral palsy. His tight muscles make his movements spastic and uncontrolled. His paralysis also affects his tongue movements, making speech impossible. But Elliot is intelligent, able to understand and learn, and very enthusiastic about life. His smile lights his entire face and conveys love and acceptance of others, disabled or able-bodied. Elliot loves the Lord and readily joins in praise and worship, moving to the music while holding his walker for support. He sings and prays aloud, using a "language" only the Holy Spirit can comprehend. Although we cannot understand the language of his grunts and utterances, it is the sweet sound of praise to God's ears. Kiarie also has cerebral palsy but is not as severely limited as Elliot. Kiarie wants to be a preacher, and even in his youth, he has shown himself to be a capable worship leader. Mariamu was born without arms. Those who don't take time to get to know Mariamu might question her ability to serve God. But Mariamu knows Jesus as her Lord and Savior, and joyfully – boldly and courageously – participates in praise and worship, raising her legs and clapping with her feet in community with others who echo her motions with their arms and hands. Mariamu uses her abilities to serve others who are more severely disabled. Holding a spoon with her toes, she gently feeds those who cannot feed themselves. She models a life lived in loving submission to the Lord. God is using each of these young people despite their disability. Their love for the Lord and joy in serving others outweighs their physical weakness.

Paul's teaching echoed God's correction of Samuel when he inspected the sons of Jesse to identify the next king of Israel: "The LORD sees not as man sees: man looks on the outward appearance, but the LORD looks on the heart" (1 Samuel 16:7). Is it possible that some Christians forget that God has chosen them, not vice versa, and reason, "of course God chose me; look at how wise, or strong, or able-bodied I am"?

Paul reprimanded the Corinthians for copying the world's ideas of wisdom and ability, glorying in man's thoughts and ideas. God says it is *his* strength and wisdom that is at work, not human. A person's inability does not limit God's power and wisdom. God can accomplish more through our weakness than we can in our strength. God equips those he calls for the tasks to which he calls them. God uses us in our weakness, pain, suffering, or disability to make us aware of our dependence on him. He is pleased to work through individuals that cultures disregard. Therefore, Paul said in 2 Corinthians 5:16–17, "From now on, we regard no one according to the flesh. Even though we once regarded Christ according to the flesh, we regard him thus no longer. Therefore, if anyone is in Christ, he is a new creation." Removal of disability is not necessary. Paul does not mean God gives the person a new (or whole) body or mind; the person is a new creation because his or her spirit is renewed – the person is born again spiritually. This is how we must view people with disabilities, whether they are believers or, as yet, unbelievers.

Paul came to the Corinthians in weakness, fear, and trembling, using speech and language, but not in persuasive words and polished speeches (2:3-4). These are characteristics that are often assigned to someone with an intellectual disability (although people making that judgment may, unlike Kiarie, be hesitant to stand before the church to give their testimony).

With these words, Paul is not displaying false modesty but sincere humility so that glory and praise go to Christ, not himself. Paul says he has the mind of Christ (2:16), who was also characterized as humble and weak. Having the mind of Christ is something every Christian ought to be able to say of themselves and display in their lives.

When Paul said the natural man cannot understand or accept the things of the Spirit of God (2:14), he was referring to people who do not know Christ as Lord and Savior. Not having the mind of Christ means a person's nature is "unchanged by grace" (Wilson, 1971) and without the Spirit of God. Having the mind of Christ has nothing to do with natural ability or a certain level of intelligence. The Corinthians thought they were wise, as do many unbelievers today. To the unsaved, Christianity is foolishness and the teaching about Christ fiction. But having the mind of Christ is not something we gain through our own learning; it is revealed to us by the Spirit of God. As was said before, having even a severe intellectual disability is not an obstacle to God; limited intellectual ability does not disqualify a person from becoming part of the family of God.

Paul's teaching is also significant to relationships we establish with others in the church, both able-bodied and disabled. Paul said, "we have the mind of Christ," meaning each believer is an equal part of the body of Christ. We are one body (cf. 1 Corinthians 12), and must resist the temptation to rank people by their physical or intellectual ability.

Paul referred to Christians as being taught by the Holy Spirit (2:13). People with a profound disability are spiritual beings, just like their nondisabled peers. The ability to verbally respond or testify to God's work in one's life is irrelevant. God's Spirit reveals truth to us regardless of our physical or intellectual status. And the Spirit speaks through our acts and our love to the spirit (or heart) of people with disabilities in ways we cannot fathom. Human wisdom and human reasoning do not give nondisabled persons an advantage; in fact, they can hinder accepting the gospel's truth. But limited intelligence or mobility does not impede the Holy Spirit's ability to engage the human spirit. Neither does having minimal intelligence mean that person is irrelevant or unimportant. We all are created in the image of God.

GOD'S TEMPLE

But I, brothers, could not address you as spiritual people, but as people of the flesh, as infants in Christ. I fed you with milk, not solid food, for you were not ready for it. And even now you are not yet ready, for you are still of the flesh. For while there is jealousy and strife among you, are you not of the flesh and behaving only in a human way? For when one says, "I follow Paul," and another, "I follow Apollos," are you not being merely human? ... For we are God's fellow workers. You are God's field, God's building. According to the grace of God given to me, like a skilled master builder I laid a foundation and somebody else is building upon it. Let each one take care how he builds upon it. For no one can lay a foundation other than that which is laid, which is Jesus Christ. ... Do you not know that you are God's temple and that God's Spirit dwells in you? If anyone destroys God's temple, God will destroy him. For God's temple is holy, and you are that temple. Let no one deceive himself. If anyone among you thinks that he is wise in this age, let him become a fool that he may become wise. For the wisdom of this world is folly with God. For it is written, "He catches the wise in their craftiness," and again, "The Lord knows the thoughts of the wise, that they are futile." So let no one boast in men. For all things are yours, whether Paul or Apollos or Cephas or the world or life or death or the present or the future—all are yours, and you are Christ's, and Christ is God's.

1 Corinthians 3:1–4, 9–11, 16–23

The theme of worldly wisdom versus God's wisdom continues through 1 Corinthians as Paul addresses the factions that developed in the church in Corinth (introduced in 1:11–18). In 3:11, Paul says no one can lay a foundation other than the one already laid, which is Jesus Christ, and identifies Christians as God's temple, God's Spirit living in them (3:16).

David W. Anderson

To ignore people with disabilities, as some churches and Christians have done, is to lay a foundation: able-bodied or minimally disabled only. The implication is that God's temple can be built only using nondisabled persons or that people with a disability are unfit for the kingdom. But since we are all sinners by nature, we cannot make ourselves fit for the temple. The temple's foundation is what is important: Jesus Christ, the unchanging Word of God. Human disability does not limit God.

Dissension and quarreling in the Corinthian church led to rivalry within the church and disrupted the intended unity. Paul lumped the parties into two groups: spiritually mature or worldly infants. The essential difference was in their diet. Paul could feed solid food to those considered mature, but to those regarded as infants, he needed to provide milk. He described the worldly infants as quarreling and jealous, which prohibited them from receiving the more nourishing food he could give to their spiritual siblings. The mature were able to dine on spiritual truths because their minds were "in the Spirit." But the infants' minds were focused on things of the world and controlled by worldly thought patterns. Thus, the infants had experienced little change in their faith and spiritual understanding because their worldly focus hampered their growth. Just as infants cannot feed on steak, these immature believers could only digest pap. Their desires being self-centered rather than Spirit-oriented resulted in a division between mature and infant believers, impacting Corinth's Church.

Will our "temple" stand up under God's inspection (3:10–15) if we restrict our construction to people who are deemed able, worthy, or valuable by the world's standards? All believers in Christ are the temple of God and indwelt by the spirit of God. No physical or intellectual test for entry into the kingdom exists; the only need is regeneration by the Holy Spirit, who draws all believers into unity as one body.

To reject someone based on earthly standards, such as not being able-bodied or able-minded, weakens or destroys God's temple. The spirit of God creates faith in and draws believers into unity as one body. This has clear implications for how persons with a disability are seen and treated by the rest of the body. God chooses those the world considers foolish, powerless, or unimportant, those whom the world looks down on. Why? To bring to "nothing" what people often consider important. Why? So that no person can boast in the presence of God. God overturns the world's values and traditions, especially those which devalue certain people as being of little or no significance. God deliberately chooses men and women the culture overlooks and abuses (the "nobodies") to expose the hollowness of people who, in their own eyes and the eyes of the world, think they are "somebodies." People may *seem* weaker because we do not see their weakness in connection with God's power. Perhaps we even see ourselves as weak, unable, or having nothing to contribute. Recognizing our weakness and dependence on God allows the Holy Spirit to exhibit his power in and through our lives.

Though the world sees people with disabilities as weak, Paul suggests that God has given them an essential role in his mission, a role that can break down human pride. All human life is sacred, regardless of culture or race, weakness (disability) or strength. Each person can praise and glorify God no matter how "weak" they appear to be to others (or how worthless and insignificant they feel). God can do more as we place ourselves, in our weakness or disability, into his capable hands – more that we can do by relying on our own perceived strength. Every human person, nondisabled or disabled, is created as God's image and has a purpose and something to contribute. Regardless of our level of physical or mental ability, we are designed to create with, relate to, and be available for others.

McIntosh (2017) applied Mark 10:13–16 to disabled or very young children who are unable to voice a profession of faith, but his comments apply to severely disabled persons of any age:

> Jesus said the kingdom belongs to these little children, to babies, to infants – to people not old enough to make a faith statement. Jesus didn't put any rules in their membership in the kingdom before saying they belong. ... They don't have to profess their faith. In fact, they don't have to make a choice, because they *can't* make a choice. ... They are there entirely by God's grace. ... God's decision to impart salvation to those who cannot make a decision on their own shows his great love and care for the least in the kingdom. (p. 81)

David W. Anderson

As we have noted before, God often uses individuals the world considers weak or insignificant to accomplish his will.

Paul described Christians as God's fellow workers, God's field, and God's building (3:9). But he rebuked the Corinthians because what they professed to believe did not match their practice. Behavior and attitude, including relationships with others, must give evidence of what Christians believe. Are all people important? Are all people savable? From God's perspective, the answer to these questions is "YES!" Are we permitted to limit our love to particular people groups? Do we have no responsibility to share Christ (in word or action) with people who are disabled? Are people with disabilities exceptions to who Jesus commissioned us to take the gospel to (Matthew 28:18–20)? The answer to these questions is "NO!"

Christians are God's temple, in whom the Spirit of God dwells (3:16). In the Old Testament, the temple was a dwelling place characterized by God's divine presence, a place where God would meet with his people. But Paul was not speaking of a brick-and-mortar building. Christians are themselves God's temple. Our lives are to be characterized by loving actions and righteousness. Prior (1985) said, "these verses in 1 Corinthians urge us to take with full seriousness *both* the certainty of eternal life *and* the scrutiny which the Lord will bring to our daily service as Christians" (p. 60).

Paul spoke of how, through God's grace, he had laid a foundation for the faith of the Corinthians by sharing the gospel with them. That foundation is Jesus Christ (3:11). As servants of Jesus Christ, Christians build on (or from) that foundation. He warned that our "building" will be judged by fire, and we will either receive a reward or suffer a loss based on whether or not our "building" survives the fire. As God's temple and workers in God's field, a Christian's task is to continue "building" the temple through good (godly) works and evangelistic endeavors. All Christians, able-bodied or disabled, are God's building and God's builders. God is the architect; we are merely the workers.

In the Old Testament, offerings brought to the temple were to be without blemish (Leviticus 1:3); to present an animal that was not acceptable was an insult to God. All believers have been reconciled to God through Christ's sacrifice and presented to God as holy, blameless, and above reproach (Colossians 1:22–23). Anyone in Christ is acceptable and will not be discarded, including those with a disability. The absence of people with disabilities in the church means the building is incomplete and, being structurally unsound, may falter. Though the world sees people with disabilities as "imperfect," God does not. Where we see disability, God sees possibility.

In Matthew 18, the disciples asked Jesus, "Who is the greatest in the kingdom of heaven?" (I suspect they actually were asking which of *them* was the greatest.) Jesus placed a child in their midst and said, "whoever humbles himself like this child is the greatest in the kingdom of heaven (and) whoever receives one such child in my name receives me" (Matthew 18:4–5). The same applies to people the world thinks are like little children because of limited intellectual ability. Being physically or intellectually challenged does not mean a Christian is not part of the temple. Paul will say in 1 Corinthians 12 that those parts of the body (or the temple) we consider weak are indispensable. God's temple is holy, and all believers are part of that holy temple. A person's physical or intellectual ability is irrelevant. Being part of that temple means that Christians, able-bodied and disabled, like that temple, are holy.

J. C. Ryle (1956) defined holiness as "the habit of being of one mind with God" (p. 35). Based on Paul's teaching that God has predestined us to be conformed to the image of his Christ (Romans 8:29), Ryle explained holiness in practical terms: meekness, temperance and self-denial, love and brotherly kindness, mercy, humility, and being spiritually-minded. Disability does not prevent a person from displaying these characteristics; in fact, knowing their limitations may enable them to better image Christ to others. Being able-bodied may cause some Christians to rely on their own ability rather than to draw strength from God.

In 1 Corinthians 1, Paul introduced the idea that the wisdom of this world is foolishness from God's perspective, a theme that resurfaces throughout 1 and 2 Corinthians. In 3:19, he specifically labeled self-boasting as "folly." In the world's wisdom, people with a disability, especially a severe intellectual disability, are unimportant and may be regarded as foolish. In medieval days, an intellectually impaired person might serve as a court jester to amuse the nobility. By the mid-20th century, large institutions had been created to warehouse such people. This is no longer the case, but many people still consider these individuals worthless or dispensable. If prenatal testing suggests that an unborn baby *may* have Down syndrome, the mother may be urged to "discard" the baby through abortion or by leaving the baby at the hospital. This judgment is foolishness (and sinful) and directly contradicts God's teaching that every human being is created in (as) his image and is, therefore, a person of worth. Truly wise people are those who intentionally oppose the wisdom of the world and acknowledge that "who" we are and the gifts and abilities we have, no matter how limited they may appear to be, are nonetheless gifts of God's grace.

God does not determine a person's worth by their outward appearance (1 Samuel 16:7). Here, Paul quoted Psalm 94:11, "The Lord knows the thoughts of man, that they are but a breath," to underscore his point that God's way of thinking is not only different but far superior to that of humankind. Therefore, we do not boast, or glory, in men – especially ourselves. Even Christ did not seek his own glory but willingly subjected himself to the will of the Father. Prior (1985) wrote, "it is totally out of place to boast about people and things which … have been placed in our laps by a lavishly generous God" (p. 61). That what we have is from God's grace ties to the fact that we belong to Christ. And the believer's relationship to God, and the blessings that flow from that relationship, means we have nothing to boast about regarding salvation or our achievements. Intellectual or physical ability is irrelevant. God's gracious gift is at work in both able-bodied and disabled to bring us to salvation. As Paul wrote in Ephesians 2:8–10, we are saved by grace through faith, which itself is a gift from God, not something we can work to become or to do. Able-bodied or disabled, we are God's workmanship, created to join Jesus in his work, to engage in the good work he has prepared for us – and prepared us for.

PROMOTING UNITY

Therefore let anyone who thinks that he stands take heed lest he fall. No temptation has overtaken you that is not common to man. God is faithful, and he will not let you be tempted beyond your ability, but with the temptation he will also provide the way of escape, that you may be able to endure it. [14]Therefore, my beloved, flee from idolatry ... "All things are lawful," but not all things are helpful. "All things are lawful," but not all things build up. Let no one seek his own good, but the good of his neighbor. Eat whatever is sold in the meat market without raising any question on the ground of conscience. For "the earth is the Lord's, and the fullness thereof." If one of the unbelievers invites you to dinner and you are disposed to go, eat whatever is set before you without raising any question on the ground of conscience. But if someone says to you, "This has been offered in sacrifice," then do not eat it, for the sake of the one who informed you, and for the sake of conscience – I do not mean your conscience, but his. For why should my liberty be determined by someone else's conscience? If I partake with thankfulness, why am I denounced because of that for which I give thanks? So, whether you eat or drink, or whatever you do, do all to the glory of God. Give no offense to Jews or to Greeks or to the church of God, just as I try to please everyone in everything I do, not seeking my own advantage, but that of many, that they may be saved ... Be imitators of me, as I am of Christ.

1 Corinthians 10:12–14, 23–33, 11:1

The first 13 verses of 1 Corinthians 10 deal with what Prior (1985) called the danger of presumption, specifically the assumption that we have moved beyond certain temptations as Christians. Verse 12, "let anyone who thinks he stands take heed lest he fall," is both a chastisement of and a stern warning to those in the church who think they are flourishing in their Christian life solely through their own effort. Paul's caution about feelings of super-spirituality may also imply underlying competitiveness, leading some in the church to judge themselves to be "better" or more spiritual than others.

It is unlikely that Paul specifically had disability in mind as he wrote these words, but his warning applies to adopting an attitude of superiority over people who live with a disability or the presupposition that being able-bodied makes a person more worthy of God's love and grace. The warning to "take heed lest you fall" is aimed at spiritual attitudes but, in the context of disability, could also be taken literally: a fall could easily result in a disability. Self-pride does not shield a person from becoming disabled. The encouragement to flee from idolatry (10:14) includes running from self-idolatry – pride in our ability and accomplishments. Such a posture can morph into discrimination against and separation from individuals and families dealing with disability.

Paul attributed the divisive factions among the Corinthian believers to the absence of godly love for one another, coupled with an abundance of self-love. Matthew 22:36–40 records Jesus's response to a question about which commandment is the greatest. Jesus quoted the Old Testament instruction to love God and to love your neighbor as you love yourself (Deuteronomy 6:5; Leviticus 19:18), tying the two thoughts together: loving God requires and is demonstrated by loving our neighbor. But sometimes, our idea of "neighbor" is restricted to persons or groups like us. People with a significant disability may then be consciously or unconsciously excluded from the category of neighbor. Some people may verbally keep them at a distance, talk around them as if they are not there, avoid them altogether, or complain about their presence in the church. But fellow believers with whom we gather for worship are our "neighbors" (really, our brothers and sisters in Christ), and we are to love them without regard to their ability or disability. Concern for their best interest is essential.

Loving our neighbor is a necessary and essential outgrowth of loving God. 1 John 3:18 indicates that love must not be just words or talk but in deeds and truth. Godly love flows from unity and oneness in the body of Christ while at the same time strengthening that unity and oneness. All believers, whether able-bodied or disabled, share in Christ. This communion or participation unites us as believers.

We can all agree with Paul's statement that temptations are common (10:13), but there is no direct connection between temptation and disability. Someone may be tempted to climb a tree but lose their grip, fall, and become disabled. The disability is the result of gravity and natural consequences, not the temptation. Paul says God will faithfully provide an escape *from the temptation* but not from the consequences. Some naively believe Paul to be saying God will remove a disability if we pray earnestly, but Paul's focus is on temptations and problems, not disability. From God's perspective, disability is not a problem. Paul wrote in Romans 8:28–29 that for those who love God and are called according to his purposes, God works all things together for good – "good," meaning useful or beneficial. Paul is not saying that all things, in and of themselves, are good in the sense of being advantageous, but for believers, they are good in an ultimate sense (Beates, 2012). We may not regard becoming disabled, or birthing a child with a disability as something "good" in the sense of being desirable. Still, God can use this in a way that ultimate good results including, but not limited to, their being spiritually conformed to the image of Jesus. Disability, or the circumstances that may lead to becoming disabled, is not the result of "bad luck." God may not be the direct cause of a person's disability, but God is sovereign over the factors that led to the disability.

Disability is not stronger than God, and God's promise cannot be voided by disability. God's perfect plans and the way he accomplishes them may not be what we expect, but they can still lead to "good." Joni Eareckson Tada's paralysis, for example, was not an unfortunate accident from God's perspective. God is omniscient and was not caught off-guard when she became paralyzed. God chose not to cure Joni's paralysis but to use her, a person with a disability, to bring glory to himself and grace and salvation to many disabled people worldwide through the ministry of Joni and Friends (www.joniandfriends.org). Her paralysis, coupled with her faith in a loving, gracious God, has led to hope being brought to many disabled individuals and their families. God has a reason for allowing things we may find undesirable to enter our lives, such as becoming disabled, but he is not required to explain why he permits them. We are obligated to trust God and follow wherever and however he leads. And Christians who are nondisabled must welcome, accept, and include persons living with disability as our brothers and sisters in the Lord. Wright (2004) wrote,

David W. Anderson

"The battle for the mind remains central to the church's task in this and every age (and) has to be fought inside the church as well" (p. 107). In our context, this means battling to break through prejudicial attitudes toward persons with disabilities and affirming the potential value of incorporating them into the church body.

Paul's concern is building up and promoting unity in the church. Questions for us are: Am I building up the body of Christ? Am I thinking of the welfare of others or only myself? Are there certain people I exclude from the scope of my love and fellowship because their disability makes me feel uncomfortable? Several principles drawn from 1 Corinthians 10 give direction in answering these questions and guiding believers in their relationship with others, including persons and families that face issues of disability:

Principle #1: Seek the good of our neighbors, recognizing that the earth is the Lord's in all its fullness (10:24, 26). This includes *all* people, nondisabled or disabled. In addressing how eating food offered to an idol could confuse a weaker believer, Paul exhorted showing concern for all fellow believers, and especially those who may not understand their freedom in Christ. For our purposes, substituting disability for food, the principle is the same: we must be sensitive to and concerned for others, both disabled and those who tend to avoid people who have a disability. The point is not to back away from a disabled person because of personal discomfort. Our concern is for both the disabled person *and* the "weaker believer" who resists welcoming or interaction with persons who are disabled. Love must be shown to both, and our task is to help the weaker believer – the one who shuns the disabled – to see persons who are disabled through God's eyes.

Principle #2: Do everything to the glory of God (10:31). Withholding the gospel and Christian love from a person who is disabled does not bring glory to God. Both able-bodied and disabled are made in God's image and are to be respected. Jesus gave his life not just to redeem nondisabled persons. "God so loved the world that he gave his only Son, that whosoever believes in him should not perish but have eternal life" (John 3:16). There is no physical or intellectual qualification of the word "whosoever." The term is all-inclusive.

Principle #3: Do not offend others (10:32). Our attitude, words, and behavior can be offensive to an individual or a family that deals with disability. The gospel's call is not limited to nondisabled persons. Believers who are disabled desire a relationship with God and with fellow believers. Just as there is no physical or intellectual requirement for becoming a child of God, there must be no physical or intellectual requirement for membership in the church, the family of God.

Principle #4: Show concern for the conscience of others (10:28–29). An absence of such concern might emanate from feelings of superiority by nondisabled persons who then convey, through words or actions, that to be disabled is unacceptable or that the disability is God's punishment for sin. Since we are all sinners by nature, why are we not all disabled? Such actions or words evidence self-pride while falsely claiming God's righteous choice of nondisabled persons as part of his family.

Principle #5: Do not seek our own advantage, but seek to please others (10:33). "Pleasing others" includes welcoming and enjoying fellowship with others, including those with a disability as equals. It means focusing on the person, not the disability. It means making whatever accommodations are necessary for that individual to be and feel welcomed as a potential believer or as a brother or sister in Christ.

Principle #6: Imitate Christ (11:1). Imitating Christ in the context of disability ministry requires taking note of how Christ responded to persons with disabilities during his earthly ministry and mirroring his attitude and actions of love and grace. Note how unhesitatingly Jesus interacted with them, even approaching and touching "a person with leprosy" (Matthew 8:1–4). By curing many disabled persons, he was not suggesting that they were unacceptable without a cure (he accepted them before he cured them). The cure demonstrated who Jesus is, but it also clarified that these individuals were fully human, acceptable (even if not cured), and lovable. A disability is not a barrier to becoming a believer; curing a disability is not a requirement for salvation or inclusion in Christian fellowship. As Christians, our aim is not to please or promote ourselves and our accomplishments but to imitate Christ, whose focus was on others. Our desire should be to please our neighbors and build them up in their faith (Romans 15:2–3).

Few churches have an active outreach to persons and families dealing with disability, and some understand such ministry as something done "to" these persons, not "with" them. Disability is not a handicap; handicaps are barriers created by nondisabled persons and by the environment. The attitude of many nondisabled persons often entails fear of disability or disabled persons. Incorrect or negative assumptions about disability lead to *attitudes* of nondisabled persons, which create a handicap and limit accessibility and fellowship. The physical layout of the first church I attended as a youth was handicapping because the worship center was on the second floor, requiring attendees to climb a long staircase to attend the services. Wheelchair users and others with a significant physical limitation were thus prevented from attending the church, as the architecture created a handicap. Similarly, the absence of braille is a handicap for those with a visual impairment. Some may argue that putting braille markings on doors or providing a braille worship folder is unnecessary because no congregation members are blind. People who are visually impaired will probably never come to the church because the church has created a handicap that potentially prevents them from attending. These are examples of the normate bias; "normal" folks with no significant physical problem can handle stairs and print material. An even more substantial handicap created by the church is a theological error: attributing disability to sin and interpreting failure to be cured as an indication of little faith or prayer on the part of the person who is disabled.

Some nondisabled persons may feel uneasy in the presence of a person who is severely disabled, but God is not embarrassed by disability. Kinard (2019) wrote, "We must remove the barriers from families with disabilities so that they can enter the full life of the Church. We do this for the sake of God, who welcomes us and who has made us for His glory" (p. 18). Disability is not stronger than God, nor does it prevent God from bringing a person into a saving relationship with him. We do not often find persons with a severe disability in the church, but it is not because they do not want to come. More often, it is because the church has not reached out to them with the gospel and with God's love nor invited or welcomed them to the church. The "handicap" to their coming to Christ is us, but "the love of the community who imitates Christ can overcome handicaps to inclusion" (Kinard, 2019, p. 77).

Paul's words in Romans 12:9–10 indicate that Christians should be characterized by genuine love and brotherly affection. This is instructive to our relationship with individuals and families dealing with disability, especially when the disability is severe or profound. Our love must be genuine, not a pretense, and given to others as freely as we give love to our physical family members. We are to show honor to others, including individuals and families dealing with disability. We are to contribute to the needs of and be hospitable to others, welcoming "strangers" into our church and home. We are to rejoice with those who rejoice, weep with those who weep, and live in harmony with one another as equals. We must not disrespect "the lowly," as many with a severe disability are thought to be. Christians must not become wise in their own eyes, thinking they are better than someone who is disabled. We must do what is honorable in the sight of all and live peaceably with all, including people with a disability. As Peterson (2002) put it, "Make friends with nobodies; don't be the great somebody" *(The Message*, Romans 12:16).

Ignoring individuals and families who face the challenge of living with a disability in a world (or a church) that prizes ability fails to reflect the immensity of God's love and mercy. Paul wrote in 1 Corinthians 16:14, *"Let all that you do be done in love."* This includes making room in our heart – and in the pew – for someone who has a disability.

In Matthew 11:28–30, Jesus said,

> Come to me, all who labor and are heavy laden, and I will give you rest. Take my yoke upon you, and learn from me, for I am gentle and lowly in heart, and you will find rest for your souls. For my yoke is easy, and my burden is light.

Jesus spoke these words to people oppressed by the religious leaders in Israel and burdened by religious rituals that provided no lasting peace, resulting in no true refreshment to their souls. Usually applied to salvation, they are also descriptive of people who daily struggle with issues of disability and face opposition or rejection from nondisabled individuals or the church. Often, they feel shunned or abandoned by Christians who view disability as a curse from God, punishment for sin, or evidence of little faith (as when they are told to pray "harder" or believe "stronger" so God can remove the disability). This lays a heavy burden on the individuals and families and underscores the need for spiritual and physical rest that comes

David W. Anderson

from fellowship with and support of others. To be like Jesus, Christians (leaders and laypersons) must be ready to help these individuals and their families find physical rest by coming alongside them in practical ways and spiritual rest through accepting, loving, and supportive friendships leading to a sense of belonging in the Christian community. As we respond this way, moving beyond our own comfort-needs, fears, and uncertainties, we will not only lighten the yoke and burden felt by the families caught up in disability, and discover that our yoke in serving them is easy and the burden light.

UNITY IN DIVERSITY – GIFTS

Now concerning spiritual gifts, brothers, I do not want you to be uninformed. … Now there are varieties of gifts, but the same Spirit; and there are varieties of service, but the same Lord; and there are varieties of activities, but it is the same God who empowers them all in everyone. To each is given the manifestation of the Spirit for the common good. For to one is given through the Spirit the utterance of wisdom, and to another the utterance of knowledge according to the same Spirit, to another faith by the same Spirit, to another gifts of healing by the one Spirit, to another the working of miracles, to another prophecy, to another the ability to distinguish between spirits, to another various kinds of tongues, to another the interpretation of tongues. All these are empowered by one and the same Spirit, who apportions to each one individually as he wills.

1 Corinthians 12:1, 4–11

Part of the problem of accepting persons who are disabled into the fellowship of the church is that people cannot fathom how being disabled fits into God's plan and God's loving grace. In addition, many people do not fully understand disability or its impact on a person's functioning. Lack of exposure to, or association with, someone who is disabled may lead to the assumption that the person is more limited than he or she is. This raises concern about possibly doing something wrong or harmful when attempting to assist the person. Even being given the results of an educational, psychological, or medical assessment may offer little or no help in grasping the impact of the disability on an individual and may be misunderstood by persons not directly involved with the individual and the family. That can lead to discomfort (or fear) when approaching an individual or family dealing with disability. Nevertheless, Christians must be open to developing a relationship with the person and his or her family. Paul's instruction in 1 Corinthians 16:14 is that all we do must be done in love.

Often, when encountering someone who is disabled, the first thought, if not to walk away, is to offer to pray for the person. But Morstad (2018) wisely asked,

> Which is easier to pray? "God, take away that person's disability," or to pray, "God grant me patience when I deal with people who have different abilities, grant me acceptance of everyone, even those whose appearance disturbs me; grant me a voice to speak up for those who cannot speak for themselves, and grant me the wisdom to learn from those who have so much to teach me?" (p. 10).

For many, a prayer that God would remove the person's disability is easier and can assuage one's conscience. To pray that the person is cured may help make persons feel good about themselves, assuming that their prayer has helped meet the needs of the disabled person. But to stop at praying for a cure or for God's blessing on the person who is disabled does not build a relationship. It may actually raise a barrier between the pray-er and the disabled individual and his or her family. Spiritual depression in the person who has a disability or their family may result, as they assume they have insufficient faith or have offended God in some unknown way. And, by not investing time to build a relationship with the person who is disabled, the nondisabled person will miss out on the blessing that person can be to them or on what God can teach them through that person. It may also deny the person who is disabled the opportunity to share their spiritual gift.

In 1 Corinthians 12:1–11, Paul speaks of varieties of gifts, services, and activities entrusted to every believer, whether able-bodied or disabled, by the same Spirit and Lord. That Paul does not speak of *abilities, skills,* or *talents* helps us understand that since it is God who gives the gifts and empowers us to use them, the physical or intellectual status of the Christian is not an issue: God can work in and through anyone regardless of their ability or disability. As Morstad pointed out, "scripture abounds with ordinary people in ordinary places living very ordinary lives, all touched and changed forever. Today, the Spirit still seeks a place in the ordinary" (p. 98). This includes "ordinary" people who happen to have a disability. That Paul did not speak of varieties of *missions* is also significant. Christians have different gifts and different callings, but one mission: God's mission, to which we bear witness through our own changed lives and living out the great commission of Matthew 28:18–20.

God's gifts are not limited to people the world considers "able." Instead, "the many gifts of the Spirit are manifested through all members of the body, regardless of their ability or disability" (Yong, 2011, p. 94). God often uses people the world perceives as weaker or less able so the glory goes to him, not the person. Paul explained that the gifts of God are distributed liberally and graciously to believers by the Holy Spirit. This distribution is not limited to people who are nondisabled. Church leaders do not assign gifts to people, but they need to be vigilant in helping all believers identify what gifts they have received from the Spirit and ready to help them cultivate and use those gifts so that the whole church will flourish. They must not assume that a person who has a disability has no spiritual gift. A person's disability results in interacting with the world differently, but this does not mean the Spirit overlooked them in distributing gifts. The varieties of gifts, services, and activities Paul identified (12:4–6) are generic. We must not too narrowly define what we traditionally recognize as gifts or be blind to gifts the Spirit has given to believers who are disabled, even severely disabled. Elenka is a young woman in Serbia alongside whom I have ministered. Despite having a significant physical disability, she is a gifted artist, helps lead worship through singing, and has served on the staff of a small Bible school. Elenka readily uses her gifts to help me and others see the glory and love of God.

Wolfe and Spangler (2018) wrote, "God chooses to work through disability to change both hearts and minds. God does this by revealing his power through disability" (p. 59). The Spirit of God determines the type of gifts each believer has. Churches that ignore individuals with a disability and their spiritual gifts will find themselves and their church lacking.

The gifts distributed sovereignly by the Holy Spirit vary in kind, purpose, and results. In Ephesians 4:7, Paul referred to the gifts as "graces," apportioned to every believer as God determines appropriate. The gifts are not for the individual; they are for the benefit of all (for the common good, 12:7). Thus, no one can say of himself or conclude for others that they have no spiritual gifts, rendering them useless in God's kingdom. God's sovereignly allocating the gifts and placing each person within a local church is an indication that God wants those gifts to be used to establish and strengthen his church. Each person is designed and gifted for a unique ministry, but we must not limit "ministry" only to certain types of activities. Again, *every* believer has at least one spiritual gift; a particular degree of physical or cognitive ability is not required. Jesus said God can raise up children for Abraham from stones (Matthew 3:9). If God can do this with stones, he can also raise mighty warriors to do his works from people who are severely disabled. Morstad (2018) emphasized that "without ALL people being present and using their giftedness, the church should feel incomplete" (p. 621). This includes people who are disabled.

Our vision often focuses on the disability, leading some to assume the person has no spiritual gift, an assumption that runs counter to Paul's teaching. Instead, we should help that person to discern his or her spiritual gift(s) and creatively find or design ways those gifts can be exercised within the body of Christ. Even many nondisabled believers feel they have been overlooked in the distribution of gifts from the Spirit, partly because they compare themselves to people whose gifts are more visible or demonstrative, such as preaching/teaching, singing, or evangelism. But they may also feel lacking in gifts because many churches do not address the issue of spiritual gifts. This reinforces the narrowness of our vision, such that we fail to consider and look for spiritual gifts in people with disabilities, especially if the disability is severe.

In 1 Peter 4:10, the apostle wrote, "As each has received a gift, use it to serve one another, as good stewards of God's varied grace." Some understand this verse to mean not every Christian has received a gift, limiting the words "as each" to refer to only some believers. But the "each" is not limited to certain people. The Contemporary English Version (American Bible Society, 1995) captures the more inclusive meaning: "Each of you has been blessed with one of God's many wonderful gifts to be used in the service of others. So use your gift well." Thus, our Christian brothers and sisters who are disabled (even severely) also have a gift to share and must be allowed to use that gift, even if their gift is only a smile communicating love and acceptance (e.g., Nouwen's Adam, Soila, and

Elliot, mentioned previously). The gift, when exercised and welcomed, helps both the giver and receiver to know grace.

At least one spiritual gift is given to every believer, but Paul did not rank the gifts in importance. Any believer, disabled or nondisabled, who feels "gift-less" denies Paul's teaching. This may result from 1 Corinthians 12:1–22 being neglected in teaching and preaching because the gifts are defined too narrowly, because the church has been lax in helping believers to expect and identify their spiritual giftedness, or because the church has assumed persons with a disability are ineligible for spiritual gifts.

Paul said "*to each*" believer is given a manifestation (gift) of the Spirit (12:7). To be spiritually gifted, faith is necessary, but physical or intellectual soundness is not. The spiritual gifts are in addition to, and perhaps build upon, innate talents, abilities, and interests designed into each individual by God (cf. Psalm 139:13–16). These gifts are given for the common good, indicating that they are to be used, not buried for safekeeping, as was done by the "wicked and lazy" servant in Jesus's parable (Matthew 25:14–20).

In 1 Corinthians 13, Paul will point out that the gift of love sustains all spiritual gifts; without love, the rest of the gifts are nothing. "While the gifts of the Spirit are a *means* of grace, divine love is *grace itself*" (Wilson, 1971, p. 195). The gift of love is not exclusive to nondisabled people. People with a severe physical or intellectual disability are often more "naturally" loving than their nondisabled peers. Paul's teaching about the resurrected body (1 Corinthians 15) brings a future hope to all people. But the church should be a place of hope even now, openly welcoming individuals and families facing issues of disability into fellowship and encouraging them in the use of their Spirit-given gifts. To exclude a person with a disability, assuming they have no spiritual gift or usefulness in the church, does not demonstrate the love which is to characterize every Christian. Yong (2011) asserted:

> The many gifts of the Spirit are manifested through all members of the body, regardless of their ability or disability. In fact, it is more in keeping with Paul's theology of weakness that the more powerful manifestations are mediated through those whose abilities are less noticeable or are thought to be lesser candidates for God's work

David W. Anderson

from a worldly or "normal" point of view … The Spirit distributes gifts liberally and graciously so that people with disabilities are just as capable – if not more capable – of contributing to the edification of the community of faith, and hence are necessary in that sense (p. 94).

Just all parts of the body of Christ are essential (as Paul shows in 1 Corinthians 12), so are opportunities to use one's spiritual gifts. Churches must recognize this and allow members with a disability to serve the body as they are able. To limit any believer's ability or opportunity to share the gifts the Spirit has bestowed, we also limit the church's witness in the world.

UNITY IN DIVERSITY – ONE INTERDEPENDENT BODY

For just as the body is one and has many members, and all the members of the body, though many, are one body, so it is with Christ. For in one Spirit we were all baptized into one body – Jews or Greeks, slaves or free – and all were made to drink of one Spirit. For the body does not consist of one member but of many ... The eye cannot say to the hand, "I have no need of you," nor again the head to the feet, "I have no need of you." On the contrary, the parts of the body that seem to be weaker are indispensable, and on those parts of the body that we think less honorable we bestow the greater honor, and our unpresentable parts are treated with greater modesty, which our more presentable parts do not require. But God has so composed the body, giving greater honor to the part that lacked it, that there may be no division in the body, but that the members may have the same care for one another. If one member suffers, all suffer together; if one member is honored, all rejoice together. Now you are the body of Christ and individually members of it.

1 Corinthians 12:12–14, 21–27

Paul has already raised the issue of favoritism in the church at Corinth, by which certain people or groups are valued, and others demeaned. In 1 Corinthians 1 and 3, Paul faults the Corinthians' ideas or loyalties which have created divisions in the church, pointing out that "the wisdom of this world is folly with God" (3:9).

Worldly wisdom is evident when nondisabled people elevate themselves above people who have a disability, especially if that physical or intellectual disability is severe. Such "wisdom" reveals the pride of the nondisabled, which prevents those with a disability from being seen and accepted as equal parts of the body of Christ and from recognizing spiritual gifts given to believers who have a disability. As a result, the attitudes and actions of nondisabled believers may cause disabled believers to feel "less honorable" and "unpresentable." 1 Corinthians 12:12–14 and 21–27 address this issue.

The theme of strength through weakness frequently surfaces in both epistles to the Corinthians. In 12:22, Paul refers to parts of the body that *seem* weaker, which implies that some in the body of Christ judge themselves as being *stronger*. This assessment, and the divisions that result, stem from the worldly thinking Paul has rejected. This prejudicial thinking is the reverse of God's valuation: those who appear to be weaker, God sees as essential.

Making an analogy to the human body, Paul explains that all parts of the church body are necessary; none is to be excluded or demeaned. The parts that seem weakest and least important Paul identifies as indispensable (12:22) – not only are they needed, we cannot do without them. Though our physical "parts" have different functions, they all belong to our body: "God has so composed the body, giving greater honor to the part that lacked it, that there may be no division in the body, but that the members may have the same care for one another" (12:25–26). In short, the various parts of the body are interdependent. Because some parts of the human body cannot be seen without advanced medical technology – the heart, liver, and kidneys, for example – we forget how essential they are, only attending to them when a physical problem arises. But for our "more presentable" parts – face, hands, and manner of speaking – time and money are willingly expended so that we present a good image to others. Paul's analogy of the human body to the church body is clear. It applies to welcoming and including in the church individuals and families dealing with disability. We wear clothing to hide our "unpresentable" parts. But we must not regard people with disabilities as unpresentable and hide them away.

People with a disability are visible, but we easily miss the inner beauty and gifts they possess if not seen with the heart. To assume that people with a disability have no beauty or gifts which can benefit the church deprives both those with disabilities and those who are nondisabled the opportunity to serve and fellowship with the whole church body. Some shy away from persons with a disability because they lack knowledge about disability, which leads to personal discomfort or fear. For many nondisabled persons, disability suggests a "negativized form of human dignity" (Swinton, 2012, p. 177). God, however, does not see people with disabilities as being unimportant, or less important, parts of the body of Christ.

Paul's assertion that the church is to be a place marked by harmony and mutuality counters the divisions caused by attitudes toward people with a disability. He describes the weaker, less presentable parts of the church body as essential to the body. No one is unnecessary or unimportant; just as we need all our physical body parts to be "complete," we need one another to be complete. Interdependence, a principle evident in our physical body, is also an essential characteristic of the church body. Interdependence emphasizes community, but not uniformity. Interdependence is "the core of the very definition of God's people (Petersen, 1993, p. 34). The church, as an inclusive community, should be characterized by recognition and encouragement of each "body part," including those considered severely disabled. Roles played by each member will vary, just as their spiritual gifting varies, but each is necessary to the healthy functioning of the whole. A spirit of independence from other parts of the church body is not in accord with scripture.

An "independent Christian" is a contradiction in terms; we need Christ and the power of the Holy Spirit, but we also need one another. Interdependence was established by God in the Garden of Eden when God said – not as an afterthought, but for our benefit – "It is not good that the man should be alone; I will make him a helper fit for him" (Genesis 2:18). That same interdependence is to characterize the church body. Regardless of perceived strengths or weaknesses, we are all members of one body, the body of Christ. Both the weak and the strong are equally crucial for the proper functioning of the whole body. Interdependence acknowledges the uniqueness and irreplaceable nature of each part. To value and enjoy each "part" of the body of Christ involves caring for and nurturing one another, just as we value and care for the parts of our human body (12:25). Nurturing includes helping each member of the body of Christ to identify and develop the natural talents God has designed into them and the spiritual gift(s) God has graced them with, and then providing each member of the body opportunity to use these attributes to glorify God and strengthen the rest of the body.

Each member's contribution will be different depending on their ability and their gift. The contribution of some members may be more visible, but the intellectually impaired person who arranges a room for a meeting or cleans up afterward makes an essential contribution to the church, happily doing what some "important" members might feel is beneath them. Mike Cope's daughter, Megan, had a severe cognitive impairment, was medically fragile, and lived only to the age of ten. But by her presence in his life, Megan altered his world and his perception of what was important. He wrote of how Megan helped him rethink what is important and realize what truly matters has to do with the heart: keeping promises, seeking justice, and unconditional love (Cope, 2011). Chuck Colson's grandson, Max, has autism, but in the epilogue to his daughter's book, he wrote, "Max truly sees the world as God intended – he's not judgmental or impressed by looks, status, or finances, he doesn't try to 'fit in.'" (Colson, 2010, p. 190). How different our churches might look – and be – if this was true of everyone.

Interdependence includes the responsibility to care for one another. Just as we show special concern for the weaker parts of our physical body, we must offer a special concern for the "weaker" parts of the spiritual body so that each part of the body feels secure and valued. This means helping them find their "identity" as children of God and to understand their importance to the whole body. Each part of the body of Christ has a distinctive contribution to the complete body.

Being indispensable, these "weaker" members of the body bring "life" to the whole body. Those who are "strong" need to be open to learning from their weaker body parts. Those parts of the body of Christ who seem weaker may better understand the power of God because they know it is *God's* strength working in and through them, not their own. That these weaker brothers and sisters are indispensable suggests they have "power" over those who think themselves stronger because "the seemingly stronger ones cannot do without them" (McNair, 2014, p. 147). Thus, those regarded as weaker, who go unnoticed or ignored, may be most necessary to the church's welfare. Scripture contains many instances of God's use of people assumed by others (or by themselves) to be weak: Moses had a speech defect; Gideon thought he was the weakest member of his family; Mary was a young unmarried girl who became the mother of Jesus.

As Frost (2000) explained, it is not God's involvement that is limited, but our awareness of his involvement:

> We have come to believe that the extraordinary is the way in which God chooses to be revealed to us. We desire to see great displays of supernatural power or inexplicable phenomena to remind us that God is awesome and wants to be known by us" (p. 38).

We must learn to expect God to reveal something about himself in everyday life and recognize that he often does so in unexpected ways and through ordinary people, including those with a disability. Without this awareness, we miss God's working in and through people with significant disabilities, such as Elliot and Kiarie (mentioned earlier). Insisting that a disability be cured, as some churches or individual Christians do, suggests that God cannot work in or through someone who is disabled (or that we know what is best and God needs to listen to us). But God is not limited by our limitations. We must remain open to what God may be doing in, and revealing about himself through people who are disabled. To dismiss these individuals as having nothing to offer us may limit the degree to which God can show his grace and love to us through them. Becoming friends with families and individuals who deal with disability allows us to become aware of each other's gifts and strengths and the blessing they bring to our lives and churches.

Inclusion and relationship are essential elements of church membership and must be extended to all the "parts" of the body of Christ without regard to ability. The parts of our physical body do not operate in opposition to one another. Imagine the chaos that would result if a part of our physical body decided it was no longer part of the body and would no longer take orders from the brain. As the body of Christ, we are united to one another. Hamilton (2014) wrote, "We need one another the way a knee needs the rest of the leg, the way the leg needs the foot, and we must all be connected to the head, Christ" (p. 102). The church must move beyond relationships based exclusively on familiarity and being able-bodied and welcome people with a disability as fully human persons and fully part of the body of Christ (cf. Mouw, 1992).

LOVE

If I speak in the tongues of men and of angels, but have not love, I am a noisy gong or a clanging cymbal. And if I have prophetic powers, and understand all mysteries and all knowledge, and if I have all faith, so as to remove mountains, but have not love, I am nothing. If I give away all I have, and if I deliver up my body to be burned, but have not love, I gain nothing. Love is patient and kind; love does not envy or boast; it is not arrogant or rude. It does not insist on its own way; it is not irritable or resentful; it does not rejoice at wrongdoing, but rejoices with the truth. Love bears all things, believes all things, hopes all things, endures all things. Love never ends. As for prophecies, they will pass away; as for tongues, they will cease; as for knowledge, it will pass away. For we know in part and we prophesy in part, but when the perfect comes, the partial will pass away. When I was a child, I spoke like a child, I thought like a child, I reasoned like a child. When I became a man, I gave up childish ways. For now we see in a mirror dimly, but then face to face. Now I know in part; then I shall know fully, even as I have been fully known. So now faith, hope, and love abide, these three; but the greatest of these is love.

1 Corinthians 13:1-13

This passage from 1 Corinthians is well known to Christians and unbelievers alike and is often read at wedding ceremonies. Paul's concern in writing to the church at Corinth was with divisions, exclusions, and worldly wisdom, all of which demonstrate a lack of unity and love, the theme of chapter 13. Thus, the passage is very relevant to our focus on disability and the church.

Chapter 13 flows directly from what Paul wrote in chapter 12 about gifts and oneness in the body of Christ. The absence of oneness, or unity, evidences a lack of love. The various spiritual gifts discussed in chapter 12 are ineffectual in the absence of love for one another. These extraordinary gifts (tongues, prophecy, knowledge, miracles, works of charity) are also temporary, intended for this present life. Only faith, hope, and love are enduring, and the greatest, most superior, of these, is love (13:13). We know God's love for us as his children will never be exhausted, but here Paul speaks of *our* demonstration of unselfish love for others, a love which should flow readily from God's love for us. Boa (2001) described love as the greatest virtue because it is the practical application of faith and hope to our relationships with others in the present" (Boa, 2001, p. 265).

Ephesians 4:11–12 somewhat parallels what Paul wrote in 1 Corinthians 12. In Ephesians, he explained that God has given the church various types of leaders whose task is to equip the saints for the work of ministry for building up the body of Christ. The types of leaders Paul mentions are best understood as referring to categories or realms of activity rather than the relatively fixed and narrowly structured framework found in most churches today. Equipping and building up the saints is inclusive of people who have a disability. We err if we conclude that someone with a physical or intellectual challenge cannot participate in ministering to and building up others, even if that role is more passive, as with Adam's ministry to Nouwen (1997, mentioned in the context of 1 Corinthians 1:1–14, 17). Leadership in this general sense does not necessitate seminary training, nor does it require being able-bodied or intellectually intact.

Sarah Kovac (2013) was born with Arthrogryposis Multiplex Congenita, a condition that results in multiple joint contractures. She credits her parents with helping her understand the difference between *having* a disability and *being* disabled. She argues against allowing our flaws to define us or using the challenges we face "as excuses to keep us from becoming the people God wants us to be" (2013, p. 19). In Psalm 139, David wrote that God formed our inward parts and knitted us together, concluding that we were fearfully and wonderfully made (vv. 13–15). David's words apply to both nondisabled and disabled persons. For Sarah Kovac, these inspired words are comforting.

Peterson's (2001) paraphrase of Psalm 139:16 read, "like an open book, you watched me grow from conception to birth; all the stages of my life were spread out before you, the days of my life all prepared before I'd even lived

one day" (*The Message*). Geisler (2002) commented that Psalm 139:16 --
"Your eyes saw my unformed substance; in your book were written, every
one of them, the days that were formed for me, when as yet there was
none of them" -- does not simply refer to the number of days allotted to
each person, but speaks of God's care for, and providential control over, all
creation to accomplish his sovereign will and purpose. God's providence is
based on his sovereignty, omniscience, and omnibenevolence. God knows
our experience, our opportunities (and how we use or avoid them), our
growth and maturity, our present ministry, and for some, our disability.
Disability does not, and cannot, prevent God from achieving his purposes
in a person and the world. God has tasks we are to perform and has
planned and equipped us to carry out those tasks. Sometimes God's plan
includes a disability, but always, because they proceed from the heart of
a loving God, his plans are good, acceptable, and perfect (Romans 12:2).
God told Jeremiah, "I know the plans I have for you ... plans for welfare
and not for evil, to give you a future and a hope" (Jeremiah 29:11). These
truths imply – and require – a responsibility to yield to God daily and to
walk in the Spirit, even though disability may be a part of God's good
plan. Alcorn (2009) concluded from Psalm 139:16, "God knows all the
choices, free or not, we will ever make and all the consequences they will
ever produce" (p. 148). Based on Psalm 139, we know that the life of a
Christian, whether able-bodied or disabled, is a life "of absolute confidence
and security in the Lord because he is the infinite God who has created us
and who knows all about us" (Merrill, 2006, p. 589).

These truths engender confidence in Christians, able-bodied and those
with a genetic or acquired disability, and bring hope to the family. God
does not waste anything in our experience, including disability. All is for
our spiritual growth and maturity, and for the benefit of others, even if
all we have to offer is a smile (as with Soila, Elliot, and Adam, mentioned
earlier). As Kovac (2013) said, "The God who defines himself as Love will
be with me for every step ... I will always have God's love" (p. 156), and
whether able-bodied or disabled, we can share that love with others.

Whatever gifts of service we have, if not shared from a heart of love,
are fruitless and unproductive. Loving relationships and belonging are
hallmarks of the type of community the Christian church must establish
and demonstrate to the world. Paul stressed the interdependence of the

"body parts" in 1 Corinthians 12. Each part of the church community is vital to the other members of the body of Christ. To recognize interdependence and reciprocity allows us to appreciate the abilities and gifts of each person, including those who have a disability. Acknowledging and valuing each person's unique contributions to the Christian community fosters a sense of belonging, the oneness in diversity that Paul wrote about, and God has designed and equipped us for. Without openness to others, "community" cannot exist (Meininger, 2001). The same question Paul asked the Corinthians when talking about gathering for the Lord's Supper applies in the context of disability: "Do you despise the church of God and humiliate those who have nothing?" (11:22; in our focus, we can substitute "those who have a disability"). Openness to others, interdependence, and unity are essential for the church to be the *Church*. Paul's instructions in Philippians 2:1–4 bear a similar message:

> So if there is any encouragement in Christ, any comfort from love, any participation in the Spirit, any affection and sympathy, complete my joy by being of the same mind, having the same love, being in full accord and of one mind. Do nothing from selfish ambition or conceit, but in humility count others more significant than yourselves. Let each of you look not only to his own interests, but also to the interests of others.

Paul's teaching is not new. His words echo Micah 6:8, "He has told you, O man, what is good; and what does the Lord require of you but to do justice, and to love kindness, and to walk humbly with your God?" Justice, loving-kindness, and humility must characterize our relationship with others, both nondisabled and disabled.

The gifts God has bestowed among Christians are nothing without the grace of love (Wilson, 1971). All gifts of the Spirit are a means of grace, but love is grace itself. The other gifts are for this world only, but love is eternal, never coming to an end (13:8). Without love, Paul said he is nothing (13:2); he is grace-less. A love-less Christian will not attract people to the church and the gospel nor bring glory to God. The verbs Paul uses to describe love are in the present continuous tense, meaning these actions and attitudes must become a regular, prevailing practice.

Love is the central characteristic of church life and the Christian's life, requiring that Christians be delivered from discriminatory attitudes and practices so that people and families dealing with disability can be accepted and honored just the way they are (Yong, 2011, p. 118). Even the weakest members of the body of Christ (which is not a reference solely to people with a disability) are not to be undervalued or discarded by those who are nondisabled.

Rivera (2014) subtitled his book "A practical guide to loving your neighbor." His point is that compassion necessitates deliberate human contact. Being compassionate from afar amounts to doing nothing of substance. The journey of compassion for Christians begins with being a neighbor to others (Rivera, p. 12), something Jesus addressed in the good Samaritan parable (Luke 10:30–37). To properly understand "neighborliness" requires acknowledging that both nondisabled and disabled people are equally blessed with various gifts and natural talents, are equally valuable in God's eyes and are equally created in (as) God's image.

People who are disabled and people who are able-bodied are spiritual beings, having emotions, attitudes, and understandings based on their interactions with others and the world. Many individuals and families who deal with disabilities experience spiritual chaos. They seek to understand why God has allowed disability to enter their lives and what God may want them to learn about themselves and about him. That spiritual chaos often leads to an absence of hope. Existential questions may arise, like "Why am I (or this person) disabled?" or "What sin have I (or has this person) committed that resulted in disability?" Sin on the part of nondisabled persons may lead them to reject or isolate those who are disabled. Many nondisabled individuals are fearful of interacting with a disabled person. Not knowing how to assist the person and not asking for guidance from the parent or spouse, some simply turn away from or avoid interacting with the individual or the family. Confusion, demoralization, and depression of those dealing with disability, exacerbated by feeling rejected, may lead them to self-isolate. Sometimes the family may not even acknowledge the existence of a family member who is disabled. I once worked in a school where the fourth-grade teacher had a son with an intellectual disability. Her son never went to school, never left the house, and was never mentioned by his mother. If she was a believer, it is unlikely that her church would have given the assistance and welcome she and her son needed if they knew of her son's existence.

Rivera (2014) lamented that despite the church's emphasis on attracting new members, marginalized people, including those dealing with disabilities, are not intentionally reached out to by the church. We are familiar with issues of racism, and many churches seek to combat it, but ableism (prejudice against those with disabilities because of the normate bias) generally goes unchallenged by the church and may even be quietly endorsed because of the absence of a biblical view on disability. "Sharing the gospel without caring for the whole person often results in a dramatically less effective outcomes; the man or woman who feels genuinely loved, valued, and appreciated is much more likely to be open to the truths of Scripture" (Rivera, p. 175). Reaching others with the gospel is more effective when the needs of our "neighbors" are acknowledged and addressed.

Simple ways to begin reaching out to individuals and families dealing with disability can be drawn from 1 Corinthians 13. The language of love, spoken honestly and fervently *in words and actions*, will bring hope to these individuals and families: talking with and listening to them, making them feel essential to the whole body of Christ, getting to know them and their needs, being available to them, sharing space in the pew (but not by moving away from them), seeing and treating them as Jesus would.

Johnson (1989) wrote, "Christian spiritual formation is a matter of becoming the song that we sing, the Story we tell" (p. 103). The question to ask ourselves is, what song and story do we sing or tell to individuals and families affected by disability? Is it a song and story of love and welcome, or rejection and dismissal? Does our song and story lead to transformation in our own lives, as well as the lives of those individuals and families? If this is not our song and story, are we singing and telling the true gospel of reconciliation, community, belonging, love? How are our song and story flavored by Paul's teaching in 1 Corinthians 13? How does our song or story reflect the song and story of Jesus?

GRACE AND VULNERABILITY

For I am the least of the apostles, unworthy to be called an apostle, because I persecuted the church of God. But by the grace of God I am what I am, and his grace toward me was not in vain … Therefore, my beloved brothers, be steadfast, immovable, always abounding in the work of the Lord, knowing that in the Lord your labor is not in vain.

1 Corinthians 15:9-10, 58

The English word "grace" translates the Greek word *charis* and refers to God's free, unmerited, and undeserved favor. In Ephesians 2:8-9, Paul explained that it is by grace that we have been saved through faith, making faith a gracious gift from God. We are God's workmanship. Paul acknowledged this, saying he is what he is by God's grace (15:10).

But grace is not something in which we simply "stand," nor is it something we keep to ourselves. Instead, we are a conduit through which God's grace flows to others. In Colossians 4:6, Paul said our speech (communication) should always be gracious; we do not rest in grace. Grace is how we are to live. But graciousness is not limited to our words; it applies to our whole lifestyle. How we live, interact with, or react to others must be characterized by kindness, courtesy, and graciousness. As part of our witness to others, our attitude and interactions toward others should model God's grace and loving-kindness, giving joy to others, especially those often looked down upon, oppressed, or disregarded because of disability. To do this is to model Jesus in gracious actions and words (cf. Luke 4:22).

When Paul says, "I am *what* I am," he is referring to his character, attitude, and behavior toward others, both Christians and nonbelievers. The love and grace Paul received from Christ shaped his lifestyle and his concern for others. In the same way, love and grace should alter how we view people – in our focus, especially those who have a disability. Christ's grace, being operative in our lives, should create room for people with disabilities in our fellowship. Disregarding or disallowing people affected by a disability from our churches and evangelistic outreach reflects able-bodied pride, not graciousness.

Some may question whether allowing a person to be or become disabled is an act of grace on the part of God. But this question is more focused on the limitations associated with the disability than on the person. Beneath their question lies a fear of disability and how becoming disabled might alter their life. All people, nondisabled or disabled, are created in the image of God (Genesis 1:26–27). Disability neither destroys nor diminishes the image of God. Eiesland (1994) referred to Jesus as "the disabled God," a metaphorical way of thinking of Christ that can deepen our understanding of God's redemptive love and grace. Our Lord and Savior was broken, disabled as it were, to bring about salvation for humankind. Despite bodily woundedness, the image of God never loses "the wholeness of the divine in whose image the human being is made" (Longchar, 2011, p. 43).

Paul declared that all humans are God's workmanship, created to do good works that God has prepared beforehand for them to do (Ephesians 2:10). God has designed every individual (Psalm 139:13–16) and, as Paul said in 1 Corinthians 12, has given at least one spiritual gift to every believer, nondisabled or disabled. God expects that those gifts and abilities are used wisely and responsibly in service to him and in serving others. We are in error if we presuppose that disability means the person has nothing to offer, no gift or talent in their "design." Nondisabled persons must not assume that they are better or stronger in ability or spirituality than a believer with a disability. God's definition of human value and what makes a life productive is vastly different from the world's idea. There are many examples in scripture of God's using weak and unexpected people to accomplish his will, including a child named David who slew Goliath and a servant girl who encouraged Naaman to meet with Elijah.

Labels from the medical or psychological field or the cultural arena are commonly used to refer to disability and people who have a disability. Though sanctioned by the medical or psychological field, these labels fail to capture the person's essence. They mask the person by focusing on the disability so that what we see is a "disabled person" rather than a person who has a disability. Emphasis falls on the impairment and limitation, with little thought given to "possibilities." Positive attributes of the individual and the blessing that individual is and can be to others are generally left unexplored or simply ignored.

When Paul said, "by the grace of God I am what I am," he was referring to his appointment by God as an apostle, which was not something he had sought after, though his training and experience as a Pharisee were part of his preparation for this role. Christians are not apostles in the same sense as Paul, but they are tasked with proclaiming the truth of the gospel to the world (Mark 16:15). This commissioning, like Paul's, is by the grace of God.

Can a person whose body or mind is "unconventional" because of disability echo Paul's statement, "by the grace of God I am what I am?" Can a person born with a disability or who becomes disabled through illness or accident be considered an act of grace on the part of God? Disability labels draw attention to how the impairment limits the person but seldom do people look for the person's strengths and gifts. Even a severe physical or intellectual disability does not hinder God's ability to work in and through a person. God expects the talents and abilities he has designed into believers and the spiritual gifts he distributes to be used wisely and responsibly in serving him and others. It is wrong to assume having a disability means a person has nothing to offer. It is wrong for nondisabled persons to presume they are better or stronger in ability, knowledge, or spirituality merely because they are nondisabled. God's definition of human value and a productive life is vastly different from the world's definition.

In 1 Corinthians 15:9, Paul described himself as the "least" of apostles, perhaps feeling that he did not deserve to be called an apostle because he had persecuted Christians before his conversion. But then he proclaims in 15:10, "by the grace of God is am what I am." We can all echo that statement; our salvation is not the result of being "good" but is purely the result of God's grace and love. At times when we are more aware of our failures, we may ask, "who am I?" But as children of God, our status does not change because we are weak or disabled.

Cordell Brown is a man I have served in Africa, helping churches understand more about disability and the need for the church to reach out to people who are disabled. Born with cerebral palsy, the doctors told

Cordell's parents he would never achieve success and probably suggested they place him in an institution. Being Christians, his parents rejected the doctor's recommendation and listened instead to God. Years later, when Cordell wrote his autobiography, he chose for its title the words of 1 Corinthians 15:10, "I am what I am by the grace of God" (Brown, 1996/2003). And what he is, is a successful man, the creator of Echoing Hills Village, a group of homes and camps that provide appropriate and accessible recreational, residential, vocational, and educational services for persons with intellectual or developmental disabilities, mostly in Ohio, but also in Ghana. In his autobiography, Cordell related how his interest in becoming a pastor was dismissed by others. Some said his desire was admirable but that he should preach to "his own people," meaning others with a disability. The president of a Christian college, noting his cerebral palsy, considered him not to be college material and told him "Some people are just called to pass out tracts" (Brown, 1996/2003, p. 64).

Several decades have passed since Cordell received this "advice," but many who call Christ their Lord may entertain similar thoughts when meeting someone who has an obvious disability. Cordell rejected those judgments and, in the strength and grace God provided, went on to fulfill his dream. He readily and effectively uses his *abilities* to lead and teach others, recognizing that they too are what they are by the grace of God. Their disability does not define them nor restrain them from serving the Lord and leading others who are open to receive the gift they are and can be to all of us.

Disability of body or mind does not hinder God's grace from entering a person's soul. A person's disabled status does not limit the Holy Spirit. Kinard (2018) wrote that disabilities do not embarrass God and urged the removal of barriers prohibiting individuals and families who deal with disability from entering fully into the life of the church, adding, "We do this for the sake of God, who welcomes us and who has made us for His glory" (p. 18). People with a disability are not mistakes in God's creation or providence. Fallen human minds may see them as "rejects," but how we treat others should honor the gift of how God has made each person, whether able-bodied or disabled. "We must not exclude people with a disability from church, but do all we can to bring them into the anticipation of this future joy that we will all share" (Kinard, p. 34).

Consider this: Jesus made himself vulnerable by his incarnation, just as all humanity is vulnerable. At his crucifixion, he became "paralyzed," unable to move other than to turn his head from side to side and push himself up with his feet to breathe. Is it possible that a person with a disability is more openly vulnerable, better "images" God than people who are nondisabled? Personal weakness or disability may provide a greater opportunity to experience God's presence. To say "I am what I am by the grace of God" is both a confession of faith and a proclamation of usefulness. But it does not suggest that nondisabled persons are superior to those with a disability. Paul did not say this in lament, but in thanksgiving to God who created, gifted, and graced him – and us – to do God's work and bring God glory.

"By the grace of God I am what I am" includes, on Cordell's part, his disability. All that God has accomplished in and through Cordell's life is by God's grace. Without disability and the opposing views, comments, and taunts Cordell may have endured, he might never have accomplished all that he has. Disability shaped his life. Because of his own disability, his focus and his life have been oriented toward others with a disability. As a minister, a missionary, a camp-creator – all the result of God's grace – he is what he is. And what he has accomplished is by the grace of God. Too often, people see only *dis*-ability rather than the possibility disability offers or the opportunities to serve.

Grace is not just God's inclination to do good for us when we don't deserve it. Grace is the choice of, and power from, God to make good things happen in us, for us, and through us (Piper, 2021).

Paul wrote, "Therefore, my beloved brothers, be steadfast, immovable, always abounding in the work of the Lord, knowing that in the Lord your labor is not in vain" 15:58). In a devotional based on this verse, Tozer (1981) acknowledged that ministers often struggle when their ministry seems fruitless. But, said Tozer, the minister "is required to rejoice in God as certainly when he is having a bad year as when he is seeing great success, and to lean heavily upon Paul's assurance that 'your labour is not in vain in the Lord.'" Some church workers who strive to minister to and with persons who are disabled may feel that their efforts are futile, especially if the persons with whom they minister are severely physically or intellectually disabled. Our vision cannot see what God may be doing in the heart of those individuals, and there may be times when we feel our efforts are misspent. But God sees the heart of the persons we are ministering to, and God sees our heart. We might be surprised in heaven when someone whose apparent lack of understanding and response comes up to us to say "thank you" for caring, for sharing, for loving. Perhaps they might say, "but for the grace of God which you shared with me by sharing your life and time" ...

GOD OF ALL COMFORT

Paul, an apostle of Christ Jesus by the will of God, and Timothy our brother, to the church of God that is at Corinth, with all the saints who are in the whole of Achaia: Grace to you and peace from God our Father and the Lord Jesus Christ. Blessed be the God and Father of our Lord Jesus Christ, the Father of mercies and God of all comfort, who comforts us in all our affliction, so that we may be able to comfort those who are in any affliction, with the comfort with which we ourselves are comforted by God. For as we share abundantly in Christ's sufferings, so through Christ we share abundantly in comfort too. If we are afflicted, it is for your comfort and salvation; and if we are comforted, it is for your comfort, which you experience when you patiently endure the same sufferings that we suffer. Our hope for you is unshaken, for we know that as you share in our sufferings, you will also share in our comfort. For we do not want you to be unaware, brothers, of the affliction we experienced in Asia. For we were so utterly burdened beyond our strength that we despaired of life itself. Indeed, we felt that we had received the sentence of death. But that was to make us rely not on ourselves but on God who raises the dead.

2 Corinthians 1:1-9

This passage seems a bit cumbersome because Paul repeats the word "comfort" ten times in one form or another and refers to afflictions and suffering six times, all within nine verses. Paul's concern is with human suffering of any kind, but he explains that suffering, affliction, and weakness understood within the context of the gospel become a channel for God's power to be released – a point which Paul will address more directly in 2 Corinthians 12.

The context of 2 Corinthians 1 is Paul's own experience. We may not have shared suffering of the same kind as Paul, but we all know suffering and weakness as part of life, although people may define "suffering" differently based on personal experience. And we all know what it means to be comforted (although that, too, will be based on personal experience). Here, our emphasis is on the implications of Paul's teaching to our focus on disability.

The letter is addressed to the church in Corinth and all believers in Achaia, the western part of Greece (1:1). Paul's greeting to the church was both a prayer and a blessing: "Grace to you and peace from God and the Lord Jesus Christ" (1:3). Part of God's grace and peace is comfort. God is described as the Father of mercies (compassion) and the God of all comfort (1:3–4). In 1:6, Paul connected suffering with comfort, which would not be our immediate thought, but is essential to his thesis. He maintained that his affliction is for the comfort and salvation of the Corinthians and all believers; ultimately, his being comforted is for their (our) comfort. Patient endurance amid trials rests on knowing that God can bring about good through what we perceive as a bad experience, even a persistent situation. He explained that along with the trials and tribulations God allows in our lives, we also receive comfort flowing from God's grace and peace. Being a Christian means acting as Christ did, trusting the Father during struggles, and knowing the blessing that will ensue to all who follow Jesus. We also trust that God has a good purpose for what he allows in our lives, even if we do not fully understand that purpose. We trust God during our difficulties, believing that, just as Christ's suffering brought blessing to those who follow him, God can bring comfort and blessing to us as we endure various struggles and suffering.

However, the blessing of God's comfort is not meant to make its home in us; it is to be dispensed through us to others. We share *in* God's comfort so that God's comfort can flow to others who need comforting: *from* God, *through* us, *to* others.

As Christians, we are united to Christ, but we are also united to one another; the church is one body. Knowing this impacts how we look at others and understand our role in the church and the world. Rather than a building, God's "church" is "an assembly of God's people, in God's presence, to hear God's word" (Barnett, 1988, p. 26). All Christians throughout the world are the body Christ, called by and belonging to God.

David W. Anderson

This connection also extends to Paul and to all those who have gone before. God desires that we be in a loving relationship with him. The link to one another through Christ implies a "bodily" connection among believers. This connection involves loving and caring for one another.

Being in a loving relationship with God does not mean life on earth will be one of continual ease. Jesus said that we will experience tribulation in this world, but that he has overcome the world (John 16:33). Paul said there is nothing that can separate us from the love of Christ (Romans 8:25). Suffering is a part of living in a fallen world and is experienced in various forms and various degrees throughout our lifetime. Sometimes we suffer because of choices we have made, sometimes because of choices or actions of others, and sometimes our suffering is instituted by the "god of this age" (2 Cor 4:4).

Our own experience of suffering and the comfort God gives through the Spirit and other believers teaches us to be compassionate toward others. A Christian who has a disability may not experience pain or suffering because of the disability itself. But the actions (or inactions) and words of others in the church or society can create emotional "suffering" through rejection and isolation. But bodily or intellectual weakness also can create a link between the individual and the Lord, enabling them to minister out of their weakness and brokenness, even as did Christ himself. Everyone has limitations, but as we help meet the needs of others, disabled or nondisabled, we identify with them and acknowledge our dependency on God in our weaknesses. The church becomes a loving and empowering community when its members care for one another, especially those who are weak.

Any suffering which God sovereignly allows in our life is not to be wasted. Paul wrote in Romans 5:3–4 that suffering produces perseverance and character and asserted that the Spirit of God helps us in our weakness and intercedes for us, working all things together for good for those called according to his purpose (Romans 8:26-29). Allowing suffering into our lives and bringing us through that suffering is purposed by God to conform us to the image of Christ. God is sovereign over (and in) our suffering and weakness, and God is the source of comfort. Suffering, weakness, or disability are not beyond the goodness of a sovereign God who, ultimately, works in all things to bring blessing to us and to accomplish his will.

Brenner (1998) said, "Christian spirituality is uniquely developed within the context of suffering" (p. 104). God can use disability to bless us and others, bringing beauty out of disability because of his goodness, love, and sovereignty. Disability or suffering is not intrinsically good but is a means by which God can deepen our faith. God's ways often seem mysterious to us because he does not work the way we might desire, but his goal is to increase our trust in him and for us to draw strength from him. Ultimately, God's purpose for suffering, weakness, or disability is for us to learn to rely on God (1:9), not ourselves.

The world takes note of how Christians respond to pain and suffering. God can use our suffering to bring others to faith in Christ – *if* we respond correctly. The world cannot see Jesus graciously enduring his suffering or his disability as he hung on the cross. But the world can see the testimony of believers who continue in their faith, despite disability. Paul considers the sufferings and trials Christians endure to be a continuation of the suffering Christ endured as we continue with patience and trust in him. With Paul, we "fill up in our flesh what is lacking in his afflictions" (Colossians 1:24) and become that sweet fragrance or "aroma" of Christ to God.

The church is built by acts of self-denial as Christ's servants continue the work Christ began. As Christians thrive through disability or suffering, they become examples of Christ. Underlying this principle is the believer's union with Christ – Christ the Head, believers his body – a union so intimate that Christ suffers when believers suffer (cf. Isaiah 63:9). Christ's sufferings are over, but his suffering in his people continues: we share in Christ's sufferings and in his comforting (1:5).

Each person's idea of suffering or weakness will be different depending on the specific circumstances or situation, previous experiences, and their grasp of the purpose of suffering from God's perspective. Paul's emphasis, however, is not on suffering but on comforting. Suffering and disability are real. But so is comforting. As God has comforted us, we are to comfort others. Paul's afflictions and Paul's comfort contributed to the Corinthians' spiritual development and to ours. Paul shares "a dynamic way of looking at life" (Hughes, 2006, p. 26) aimed at changing how we understand suffering, and in our focus, disability.

A Christian who is disabled may feel emotionally or physically uncomfortable, aware of the weakness that disability entails, and aware of people's negative perception of disability and people who are disabled but *live* with the disability. But nondisabled persons often become uncomfortable in the presence of a person who has a severe disability, especially if unaware of the disability's causes and effects. Not knowing how to help or converse with the individual may increase the nondisabled person's discomfort. Some who would like to help may be hampered by thoughts of "what do I say?" or "what do I do?" If the person they have met has autism and displays "odd" behaviors or speaks repetitively, discomfort may increase, straining the patience of the would-be helper. Uneasiness can also result from difficulty understanding the speech of a person with a severe physical disability or from that person's physical appearance (e.g., stiff and awkwardly positioned limbs or facial expressions). Fear of incorrectly doing something may also cause a would-be helper to hesitate. Others simply move away. But these potential difficulties must not lead to non-action on the part of the church. Parents or spouses of the person who has a disability can help ease fear or hesitation in interacting. In many cases, the disabled person can let a would-be helper know if or when physical assistance is needed and how to proceed. But with a person whose disability does not limit or prevent verbal interaction, the door is open to establishing a relationship with the individual and the parent or spouse.

The comfort-giving Paul encouraged can be simply being with one another, speaking words, or taking action, altering or easing the person's mood or situation. One primary goal of this comforting is to help the person with the disability find courage and hope for the present and future, thus altering how they understand their situation and God. We have received comfort as Christ-followers. This comfort and support is to be shared with individuals and families dealing with disability, whether that of a newborn child or the result of an accident or illness. And the comfort we give, like the comfort we have received from God, will be necessary not just when the disability is identified or occurs but often throughout life. Paul said God continues to comfort us so we can continue to comfort others. We all face difficulties, but God encourages (comforts) us, sometimes through scripture, but often through other believers who share comfort and encouragement through their words and loving actions. In this sense, our suffering, difficulties, or weakness "shapes us." Having experienced God's comfort enables us to comfort others through what God has taught us and done in us through our own difficulties. Again, we are a conduit through which God's comfort flows.

Comforting others can take different forms, but it is not pity or condolence. The comfort we have received from God enables us to move on with our heart, mind, and soul strengthened or energized. Paul's specific focus was on comfort "energized" by God and suffering for the gospel. But the principle of comforting others applies to people and families who deal with disability and may be struggling to understand God, questioning his love, grace, and purpose. However, suffering is not caused by the disability itself; instead, it flows from spiritual and relational uneasiness and how other people, including people in the church, view, treat and respond to them and their disability.

Comforting and being comforted is not a one-directional activity, able-bodied ministering to disabled. Those who appear stronger comfort those who seem weaker, but those who seem weaker can also comfort those who appear stronger, perhaps because they can more easily attest to God's providential care and unfailing love. Even people with a severe disability preventing verbal communication can minister to and comfort those who are nondisabled.

In Christ, we need not fear our weakness because, in our weakness, we discover the sufficiency of God's grace. Paul wrote, "in our hearts we felt the sentence of death. But this happened that we might not rely on ourselves but on God, who raises the dead" (1:9). Paul emphasized how suffering works for our benefit in Romans 5:3–5, saying,

> "we rejoice in our sufferings, knowing that suffering produces endurance, and endurance produces character, and character produces hope, and hope does not put us to shame, because God's love has been poured into our hearts through the Holy Spirit who has been given to us."

Suffering, weakness, and disability help us maintain an eternal perspective rather than being overly focused on the things of the world. Paul asserts that our current circumstances, positive or negative, cannot be compared to the life to come in heaven, which is our final destiny. God's love does not always deliver us from affliction, but it does sustain us in the midst of it. Christians must hold to this eternal perspective, especially when experiencing significant trials, suffering, or disability.

Bringing comfort to others requires listening with our heart, not just ears, withholding judgment, and loving them. Our example is also critical: how we face and how we help others face struggles matters. How we respond and how we help others reflects a spiritual choice.

Jelena is a woman in Serbia I met in 2010 while serving on a team from Joni and Friends holding a retreat for families dealing with disability. She and her husband, Greg, are church leaders and have a ministry called Hana's Hope, so named because their youngest daughter, Hana, has autism. Several years have passed since I last saw Hana, but I remember her as a beautiful child who demonstrated the classic signs of autism. Jelena acknowledges that there have been struggles raising Hana, but she has come to see raising a child with autism (or any disabling condition) as a ministry. She says, "If I serve Hana as if I'm serving the Lord, in God's kingdom, this will be rewarded just like preaching to the masses that's been done unto the Lord."

James' words bear on what Paul wrote: "Count it all joy ... when you meet trials of various kinds, for you know that the testing of your faith produces steadfastness. And let steadfastness have its full effect, that you may be perfect and complete, lacking in nothing" (James 1:2–4).

Being a Christian does not prevent birthing a child with a disability or becoming disabled through illness or accident. God never promised to prevent or remove things we do not desire. But God has promised never to leave or forsake us (Joshua 1:5, Hebrews 12:5). When disability enters our life, we may try to bargain with God, often making promises we cannot keep. Some fear how friends and family (including people in the church family) will respond. Paul called God the father of mercies and the God of compassion who comforts us in our afflictions (1:3–4). Coming alongside others in love and compassion actualizes God's love as we "enact" comfort to them during their struggles and confusion. Compassionately responding to people who deal with disability will promote spiritual development, theirs and ours, as we learn to depend on the faithfulness of God.

FRAGRANT AROMAS

But thanks be to God, who in Christ always leads us in triumphal procession, and through us spreads the fragrance of the knowledge of him everywhere. For we are the aroma of Christ to God among those who are being saved and among those who are perishing, to one a fragrance from death to death, to the other a fragrance from life to life. Who is sufficient for these things? For we are not, like so many, peddlers of God's word, but as men of sincerity, as commissioned by God, in the sight of God we speak in Christ.

2 Corinthians 2:14–17

Paul asserted that through Christians, the fragrance of the knowledge of Christ spreads everywhere. This fragrance is not limited to people who are nondisabled. The aroma spread by Christians who have a disability may even be more robust than that of nondisabled people simply because they *live* with a disability. Barnett (1988) wrote, "What is important to God is not 'bigness' … but faithful and sacrificial service, based on the example of Christ himself" (p. 53). Other things that are not essential are intellectual ability, academic background, physical beauty, eloquence in speaking and being able-bodied. These attributes are unimportant because God works in and through us to reach others and bring glory to himself. They are part of how God has designed us and make believers, able-bodied or disabled, ideally suited to his purposes.

Barnett called for a balance between *speaking* the word of God and *being* the aroma of Christ (p. 56). Establishing a relationship with other people is critical, including how we relate to people and families affected by disability. The fragrance or aroma we present must not reflect feelings of superiority or mere tolerance of those thought to be weaker; it should communicate sincere love and fellowship. Only then are we a "beautiful perfume" to others, emanating a fragrance of life, love, and grace.

Paul said believers give off a sweet scent rising to God (2:14). We commonly splash on deodorant or cologne so that others are not offended by body odor. But that scent is artificial, and the aroma begins to wane from the moment we put it on. In contrast, the fragrant aroma of Christ is not only permanent but "grows" as Christ works in us, as we are conformed to the image of Christ (Romans 8:29) and transformed by the renewal of our minds (Romans 12:2). The exquisite fragrance of Christ living in us reaches out to others as we share the gospel in words and by our actions. In Ephesians 5:1–2, Paul wrote that Christians are to be imitators of God, as beloved children, walking in love, just as Christ loved us and gave himself for us as a fragrant offering and sacrifice to God.

Being a fragrant aroma starts with how we see others, especially those with disabilities. People with a disability are often "invisible" to able-bodied folks because being disabled does not fit into their expectations or because of stereotyped ideas of disability. Several years ago, while serving in Cameroon, I met with pastors and lay workers from area churches to help them understand disability and disability ministry. A team from Joni and Friends was distributing wheelchairs to people with a disability in a separate location. Pastor Gilbeth quickly left when we concluded our meeting to run to the site of the distribution. On his way, he passed James, a middle-aged man with a disability who was peddling his adult-sized tricycle, also on his way to the distribution site. Pastor Gilbeth, having recognized that James was also at the disability awareness session, quickly stopped and went back to James, whom he then accompanied to the site. When relating this incident to me, Pastor Gilbeth acknowledged that had he not been sensitized to disability through the teaching, he would not even have "seen" James.

Pastor Gilbeth's initial reaction represents a "fragrance of silence" rather than a sweet aroma. When learning that a friend has given birth to a child with a disability or has become disabled due to an accident, we often do not know how to respond. Often, would-be helpers seek an explanation for why a person is disabled, possibly more to assure themselves they are "safe" than to be in a position to offer assistance. Some would-be helpers may incorrectly assume unconfessed sin has led to the disability if the person does not repent and receive a miraculous cure, and then limit or sever communication with the individual or family. Their thoughts allow them to maintain personal equilibrium (especially if the other person's disability resulted from an accident) but are unhelpful and perhaps disrespectful to the person they seek to console. A sweeter aroma would be to simply sit with the persons affected by disability and pray with and for them. If the affected person cries out, "Why?" the best response is often silent presence rather than a theological discussion.

Often, individuals and families dealing with disabilities have limited hope, especially if they are pushed away by others (including Christians), are blamed for personal sin as the cause of the disability, or are judged as having inadequate faith. To be a pleasing aroma to them requires embodying hope and offering encouragement and assistance when appropriate. In sharing our life and love with others – believers and unbelievers, nondisabled and disabled alike – we share with them the fragrance of God's love. What actions make our offering pleasant-smelling? Verbally sharing God's love through the gospel is a start, but showing respect, being gracious, offering sincere friendship, and performing practical acts of love and kindness add to the sweetness of the fragrance. What would make our offering an unpleasant and foul-smelling aroma? Ignoring, avoiding, or rejecting people or families affected by disability, being oblivious to the person and the need, attributing the disability to sin, or reacting in pity rather than love. Believers who are critical of other Christian brothers and sisters who reach out to individuals and families facing issues of disability also raise a stench – before those they reject and before God. As we walk in love and communicate love through words and actions, we also present a fragrant offering to God, the author of our faith.

Being a fragrant aroma also relates to how people "see" us – our demeanor, words, and openness. Readiness to befriend and develop meaningful relationships with individuals and families experiencing issues of disability determines whether our aroma is sweet-smelling or malodorous. We must seek to "see" the individuals and families who struggle with disability or with people's attitudes toward disability and the person. Developing a relationship with the individual and family will help us respond with compassion (a sweet aroma) and address their questions rather than answer questions they are not asking. Building a

David W. Anderson

relationship based on Christian love will help us know the best way to respond and assist without overstepping our welcome. Being a fragrant aroma of Christ to these families is a form of "incarnational ministry," loosely patterned after the ministry of Jesus, who in his incarnation took on human form. We do not have to become disabled to minister to people with a disability, but we do need to know the persons we are ministering to and understand their physical, emotional, relational, and spiritual needs so that our "fragrance" is welcomed. Exploring the gospel accounts of Jesus's interactions with people with a disability or significant illness and modeling Jesus's actions and words can help our fragrance be pleasing.

Can people with disabilities radiate a fragrant aroma? Anastasia is a young woman from Ukraine with whom I have had the opportunity to interact and minister. She exudes, without thinking, a sweet aroma of grace and love. Though physically disabled due to childhood polio, Anastasia is a gifted artist who desires to serve and bless others through her artistry. She appears more ready and more able than some nondisabled people to share the aroma of Christ in the circumstances in which they live despite her physical limitation. Many people see only the physical disability, evidenced by Anastasia's wheelchair. But Anastasia is comfortable with who she is as a child of the King. She does not think of herself as a disabled woman but as a woman who lives with a disability.

Millar (2020) reminded readers that the proclamation of the gospel is not about us. Instead, our sufficiency for gospel ministry is based "on the fragrance of Christ, which God himself spreads through the gospel … It is about God speaking in Christ through us" (p. 50). Soila (mentioned previously) has an important ministry. Despite her significant intellectual disability and inability to speak, she radiates the sweet fragrance of the knowledge of Christ in her worship and her smile. She is a reminder that no one comes to Christ through their own strength or reasoning ability. God calls whom he will, and the Spirit of God enables a response; we merely follow. While unable to give verbal testimony to Christ's working in her life, Soila beautifully displays the joy of salvation and draws others to a more profound experience of God's presence as she engages in worship.

In the sight of God, we are, like Paul, to speak Christ in the world, using words when appropriate but "speaking" in loving action always. Paul's instruction that love must be genuine (Romans 12:9) and Peter's instruction to be clothed with humility, remembering that God opposes the proud but gives grace to the humble (1 Peter 5:5), help us understand what being a fragrant aroma before God and others entails.

Being a fragrance of life also relates to how God sees us. Does our life have an aroma of obedience, sacrificial love, willing service to others – nondisabled or disabled? Do our actions remind God of Jesus? The question before us is, do we want to be a fragrance of death or a bouquet of life?

UNVEILED FACES

You yourselves are our letter of recommendation, written on our hearts, to be known and read by all. And you show that you are a letter from Christ delivered by us, written not with ink but with the Spirit of the living God, not on tablets of stone but on tablets of human hearts. Such us the confidence that we have through Christ toward God. Not that we are sufficient in ourselves to claim anything as coming from us, bur our sufficiency is from God, who has made us sufficient to be ministers of a new covenant ... of the Spirit ... Since we have such a hope, we are very bold, not like Moses, who would put a veil over his face so that the Israelites might not gaze at the outcome of what was being brought to an end. But their minds were hardened. For to this day, when they read the old covenant, that same veil remains unlifted, because only through Christ is it taken away. Yes, to this day whenever Moses is read a veil lies over their hearts. But when one turns to the Lord, the veil is removed. Now the Lord is the Spirit, and where the Spirit of the Lord is, there is freedom. And we all, with unveiled face, beholding the glory of the Lord, are being transformed into the same image from one degree of glory to another. For this comes from the Lord who is the Spirit.

2 Corinthians 3:2-6, 12–18

Paul described the Corinthian believers as his "letters of recommendation" – letters written by the Spirit of God on the tablets of human hearts. What did he mean by this? What kind of letter were they? Certainly not a letter of recommendation for a job being sought, nor a letter from a long-lost friend to catch up on life. These letters of recommendation were letters attesting to God's spiritual change in the lives of the Corinthians believers through the Holy Spirit. We might say they are letters of *commendation,* acknowledging the impact of his ministry in their lives.

When Paul said they were "letters from Christ, written not with ink but with the Spirit of the living God, not on tablets of stone but on tablets of human hearts" (3:3), he was referring to an internal change, not a change in external appearance. The process of this transformation is not a one-time event but continues throughout life as we draw ever-nearer to God, with a true heart and full assurance of faith (Hebrews 10:22). This transformation involves learning more about God's greatness and continually growing spiritually. Being transformed to God's image or likeness is an ongoing process as our mind is renewed (Romans 12:2) and through the development and exercise of the fruits of the Spirit (Galatians 5:22–23). That process of transformation continues throughout our earthly lives, as we progress "from one degree of glory to another by the Lord who is the Spirit" (3:18). The Spirit of God is the Transformer; Christians willingly participate in this ongoing process throughout our time on earth. Some may be transformed more quickly than others, but God does not give up on us because of our slowness. Paul stressed that "he [God] who began a good work in [us] will bring it to completion at the day of Jesus Christ" (Philippians 1:6). Part of our transformation involves sharing and *living* the gospel, thereby communicating God's love to others.

Moses put a veil over his face after receiving God's law and returning from the mountain so the Israelites would not see that the "glow" of his face from having spoken with God was fading (Exodus 34:29–35; 2 Corinthians 3:12–13). But Paul wrote that Christians, with "unveiled faces," are being transformed (3:18) into the image of Christ. This transformation enables believers to display Christ to the world through our words, actions, and loving care for others. While our appearance does not actually "glow," as did Moses', our lives should glow in a spiritual sense, so the glory of God can be seen by others as we faithfully re-present Christ to the world. We still look the same physically, but through an attitude of love and confident hope, we reflect God's glory. For some believers, that transformation is evident – the change in Paul, for example. But for other believers, the transformation will be less dramatic, but our lives are changed as our hearts are changed.

Just as a veil remained over the hearts of people in Moses's day, a cover may remain over the hearts of people today, clouding the way people with disabilities are seen by others (including Christians), and even the way people who are disabled view themselves or God. But is disability a permanent, impregnable veil preventing persons who are disabled from seeing God for who he is or from being transformed into the likeness of Jesus? Do nondisabled people clutch God's grace to themselves? Do we need the Spirit of God to remove the veil over our hearts that leads us to ignore ministry to people with disabilities?

Wright (2004) wrote that when Christians look at other believers, they are looking at people in whose heart and life the Lord has been actively working "to heal, to soften, to change, to give life – in other words, to give glory." Paul wants us to recognize "the life-giving spirit in the faces of our fellow Christians" (p. 38). But our attitude toward disability and people who have a disability can prevent us "from seeing the healing, life-giving light of the gospel" (p. 42) in their lives. How the church deals with and looks at disability and people with disabilities speaks to the world. It will convey either God's love and grace or Satan's lies. Is our gaze limited to the physical? Do we need spiritual x-ray vision to see the person, not the disability?

In saying, "God has made us sufficient to be ministers of a new covenant" (3:6), Paul recognizes his weakness and consequent dependence on God. But his use of the word "us" does not refer only to people who are nondisabled. Paul's confidence was not in himself or his preparation as a pharisee. It stemmed from the sufficiency of the new covenant, the Holy Spirit, and the radical heart-transformation he had experienced. That same heart transformation can occur in people with severe intellectual or physical disabilities: our disability does not hinder the Spirit of God.

That *all* believers "are being transformed into the same image from one degree of glory to another" (3:18) indicates that being physically or intellectually disabled is not a hindrance. Even the strongest and ablest of persons cannot transform themselves; transformation is God's doing. The transformation Paul spoke of is not a physical change, as from disabled to nondisabled status, but an ongoing change to becoming more like Christ.

The transformation process is not hampered by disability; in fact, having a disability may make the inner transformation more evident. Elliot and Mariamu (mentioned earlier) are two children I came to know and love when serving the Lord in Cameroon. Elliot has severe cerebral palsy, leading to awkward movements, dependence on a walker for stability, and an inability to speak. But the glory of God is visible in Elliot's exuberant prayer and worship, his radiant smile, and his enthusiastic approach to life. Mariamu was born without arms. She loves Jesus and joyfully serves more severely physically disabled children at the center where she and Elliot live. Using Paul's words, light shines through the "darkness" of Elliot's and Mariamu's disability to display the knowledge of the glory of God, both in them and through their actions. Elliot and Mariamu are not alone; Christians who have a disability "preach" either by words or through the beauty of the Lord shining in their faces and their readiness to serve others as Jesus did.

CRACKED CLAY POTS

For what we proclaim is not ourselves, but Jesus Christ as Lord, with ourselves as your servants for Jesus's sake. For God, who said, "Let light shine out of darkness," has shone in our hearts to give the light of the knowledge of the glory of God in the face of Jesus Christ. But we have this treasure in jars of clay, to show that the surpassing power belongs to God and not to us. We are afflicted in every way, but not crushed; perplexed, but not driven to despair; persecuted, but not forsaken; struck down, but not destroyed; always carrying in the body the death of Jesus, so that the life of Jesus may also be manifested in our bodies ... So we do not lose heart. Though our outer self is wasting away, our inner self is being renewed day by day. For this light momentary affliction is preparing for us an eternal weight of glory beyond all comparison, as we look not to the things that are seen but to the things that are unseen. For the things that are seen are transient, but the things that are unseen are eternal.

2 Corinthians 4:5-10, 16-18

Paul touches on the harsh realities of human existence in this passage: suffering and physical or mental decline. We know from the Acts of the Apostles and other epistles of Paul that his life was not one of comfort and ease. After his conversion, Paul experienced significant difficulties in life at the hands of his enemies and endured storms and shipwrecks (cf. 2 Corinthians 11:23–28). Though well acquainted with suffering, Paul endured it without grumbling. Being weak and fragile human beings, we all face trials and difficulties in life, including physical limitations and uncomfortable situations. Our weakness as human beings is undeniable given the fact that we all face the last enemy, death.

Paul described Christians as containing a priceless treasure: the knowledge of the glory of God in the face of Jesus Christ (4:6). But because of human weakness, we are like broken clay pots within which this great treasure is concealed. It is the treasure that is valuable, not the clay pot. Think of the Dead Sea Scrolls, hidden in clay pots for centuries before being accidentally discovered in 1947. The clay pots themselves were of minor significance, but the treasure they contained, the Dead Sea Scrolls, is invaluable.

Christians are like those broken and fragile clay pots. Nondisabled people often hide or disguise their brokenness, but persons who have a physical or intellectual disability are unable to hide their "brokenness." Elliot's cerebral palsy, Mariamu's congenital amputation, Anastasia's physical disability, and Soila's intellectual impairment are clearly visible, but focusing on the outer container's brokenness is to miss the treasure. God made each of us the way we are, including innate disabilities and abilities, but God nonetheless equips us for the work he has for us to do. Christians should never say they lack gifts or abilities, complain about having limitations or a disability; God knows what he is doing. Psalm 139:13–15 indicates that each person's genetic structure is directly from the hands of God, who formed our inward parts and knitted us together with purpose. We are all amazingly and wonderfully woven by God according to his design and intent. We are vessels for God's use, but weak, "cracked" vessels so that God's power can be displayed as he works in and through us. One need only look at Joni Eareckson Tada to see what God can do through human weakness (Tada, 2009; Tada & Estes, 1976/2001). Our focus must be on the treasure within, not the weak outer vessel; not on ourselves as the servant, but on God as the Master.

A postal system analogy helps us understand Paul's teaching in 4:7–10. We often receive mail or packages that look important. The envelope or box may bear an official-looking seal suggesting it contains something of significance or value. But we do not prize the envelope or box; they are unimportant and are quickly torn open and discarded. It is what is inside that we value. On the *outside,* we are like that shabby envelope or battered box. But *inside,* we have the Spirit of God and the peace which comes from Christ. It is who we are as children of God that is important, not our outer appearance. When encountering a person with a severe disability, people often react to the "wrapping," the physical, intellectual, or behavioral trappings, but ignore the inner contents: a human being, and possibly a person of faith who, as we saw in 1 Corinthians 12, has natural talents and spiritual gifts, and is an indispensable part of the body of Christ.

Everyone struggles in many ways and to varying degrees. Though our struggles may not match or be to the same extent as Paul's, we can relate to his words about being afflicted, perplexed, persecuted, and struck down (4:8–10). Focusing on our struggles, difficulties, or weaknesses without considering God's presence, power, and purpose for our life can leave us feeling overwhelmed or forsaken. But God allows these trials and struggles so that we, like Paul, understand the power is God's, not our own, and so that others can see God's faithfulness in meeting our needs. We can say with Paul that we are not crushed, in despair, broken, or destroyed.

By highlighting the discrepancy between the treasure and the pot, Paul affirms that our weakness does not present a barrier to God's purposes. Our power, used in our strength and drawing on our intellectual prowess and our earthly perspective, can forestall God's intentions. Rather than being random or incidental, a Christian's suffering is of divine appointment and often contributes to the gospel's spread as we remain firm amid struggles. Hughes (2006) wrote, "It remains God's will that his frail jars of clay be used to show that the surpassing power belongs to God" (p. 93).

Sometimes people look at severely disabled persons and, believing they have no purpose, may ask, "Who are *they?*" There may also be times when we reflect on our own lives and purpose and ask, "Who am *I?*" – seeing ourselves as just a cracked or broken clay pot. But even the light generated by a candle placed inside a cracked pot shines through the cracks. When we realize our weakness as human beings, it is clear that the light is not in our "cracked pot;" it is the light of God shining into and out of our lives. Paul wrote in Ephesians 5:8–9, "at one time [we] were darkness, but now [we] are light in the Lord. [Therefore,] walk as children of light (for the fruit of light is found in all that is good and right and true)."

Severe disabilities do not necessarily lead to physical suffering, as most disabilities involve little or no physical pain. Any suffering felt by a person with a disability is more likely due to overt or covert actions and attitudes of nondisabled persons. Negative responses from nondisabled persons stem largely from incorrect assumptions about disability and fear of how their lives would be different if they became disabled, leading them to resist associating with people who are disabled. Church leaders and laity may see disabled adults as unable to contribute financially or having no gifts to share with the body of Christ, thus considering ministry to them as unimportant. Some church officials may refuse to have children with a disability participate in children's activities unless a parent stays with the child, thereby depriving the parent of the opportunity to participate in worship. As a result, individuals and families dealing with a disability may feel persecuted, ridiculed, distressed, ignored, abandoned, or worthless – instead of feeling supported and encouraged by the body of Christ. Correspondingly, several contributors to Walker's (2012) book described the prejudice and discrimination they faced when, as persons with a disability, they sought a pastoral role because of negative expectations of church or denominational authorities. Based on looking only on the outer shell (the "cracked pot"), such un-Godlike thoughts and attitudes send the message that having a disability makes a person unacceptable as part of the body of Christ, contrary to Paul's teaching in 1 Corinthians 12.

In 4:10, Paul wrote that Christians always carry in their body the death of Jesus so that the life of Jesus may also be manifested in them. In saying "the death of Jesus," Paul has in mind not just his crucifixion but the "long journey through suffering up to and including the cross" (Millar, 2020, p. 70). Weakness, suffering, or disability may characterize a person's life and ministry, but *our* strength and effectiveness in ministry and witness is not the central point; God's presence in our lives and God's empowerment in ministry is the point, whether that ministry is from a pulpit or individual witness. In Romans 8, Paul said our present sufferings do not compare to the glory that will be revealed to us (v. 18) and affirmed that the Spirit of God helps us in our weakness (v. 26). In Romans 8:28–29, Paul asserted that all things (which includes disability) work together for good for those who love God, are called according to God's purpose, and are predestined to be conformed to the image of his Son (the transformation Paul referred to in 2 Corinthians 3:18). Hence, neither suffering, weakness, nor disability is wasted; they serve a purpose. We are weak, fragile clay jars so that *God's* glory will be revealed in us. Our body (our outer self) is wasting away, but our inner self (our spirit) is being renewed daily (4:16).

Christ came to give us peace, but godly peace does not mean a life of ease. Jesus gave Christians his peace and said our hearts should not

David W. Anderson

be troubled or fearful (John 14:27). Similarly, Paul urged the Colossians to "let the peace of Christ rule in your hearts" (Colossians 3:15). Living peacefully neither implies nor demands the absence of difficulty, struggle, or disability. Instead, peaceful living flows from the confidence and satisfaction of being a child of God. Believers singled out as blessed in Jesus's beatitudes (Matthew 5:3–12) include the poor in spirit, those who mourn, the meek, the persecuted, and the reviled – words that may characterize some individuals' experience and families who contend with disability. Why are they blessed? Why should they rejoice and be glad? Not because of earthly rewards and benefits and not because of physical or intellectual ability or disability, but because their reward *in heaven* is great. Might a faithful but disabled Christian receive a greater reward because they serve Christ knowing that it is God's power working in and through them, whereas a nondisabled Christian may draw on his own strength and fail to acknowledge God?

Paul said, "we do not lose heart. Though our outer self is wasting away our inner self in being renewed" (4:16). Paul may not have been thinking about disability when he wrote of our outer self "wasting away," although his body was undoubtedly weakened from beatings he had received during his ministry, but the principle applies. Whether born with a disability or becoming disabled through accident or illness, the Christian's inner self is still being renewed (transformed). A missionary who had a vital ministry in Nairobi, Kenya, wanted to expand his ministry to include Mombasa. But while driving from Nairobi to Mombasa, he became severely disabled (quadriplegic) in a traffic accident. Because of his disability, he was no longer able to minister in Kenya. Yet, even from an iron lung during his rehabilitation in the U.S., his ministry continued, and he led some of his nurses and caretakers to the Lord. Through his weakness, through his "cracked pot," the kingdom grew.

Paul's perseverance flowed from his understanding of what God was doing in his life. But many followers of Christ go about daily life without consciously evaluating their behavioral and thought-life in terms of being a child of God and a re-presentation of Christ in the world. Paul's words in 4:16–18 characterize a positive way of living for Christians, especially those who have a disability. People with an obvious disability may find it easy to acknowledge that God works in and through them. In contrast, a thriving ministry may lead a nondisabled person to become prideful.

Elenka (mentioned earlier), the young woman who served at a Bible school in Serbia where I have frequently taught, was born with a physical disability in which her arms and legs are awkwardly positioned (somewhat twisted and "locked" so that they do not bend). Growing up in Serbia was difficult because of her disability and how nondisabled peers and adults viewed her. The limited use of her legs and arms makes walking, using stairs, and other everyday activities difficult. But Elenka is a lovely and gracious woman. She is a talented artist, despite the twisted and stiffened positioning of her arms. As a mature Christian woman, Elenka was an example to students and staff at the Bible school, where she assisted the director, served as a worship leader and monitored the students' day-to-day responsibilities in helping to care for the school. For the last few years, Elenka has chosen to live in a government-run facility for individuals who are disabled, where she continues her ministry by sharing the gospel with residents with more significant disabilities than her own. Like other Christians who do not succumb to life's problems and difficulties, Elenka reveals the life of Jesus, not in her own strength, but through what Barnett (1988) described as "the transcendent, sovereign power of God" (p. 90). Perhaps Christians living with disability more clearly embody this principle than Christians who are nondisabled.

Pastoral care is a ministry in which the entire Christian community should be engaged, not just those in leadership positions. Shelp (2003) wrote, "The congregation, not the clergy, is ultimately responsible for the care of people ... The church is formed by God to care for humanity through acts of love and mercy" (p. 32). Having a disability does not relegate a person to merely being the recipients of pastoral or congregational care. They can also be givers of pastoral care, even if severely disabled and unable to speak. Each person is unique and equally fashioned, known, and loved by God. In sharing his experience of caring for Adam, a young man with severe disabilities, educator and theologian Henri Nouwen (1997) considered being created in the image of God means. Reflecting on how God reveals himself through and in even those with severe disabilities, he wrote about Adam, a young man with a severe disability with whom he worked:

David W. Anderson

> Adam's humanity was not diminished by his disabilities. Adam's humanity was a full humanity, in which the fullness of love became visible for me ... We were friends, brothers, bonded in our hearts. Adam's love was pure and true. It was the same as the love that was mysteriously visible in Jesus, which healed everyone who touched him. (pp. 50–51)

Adam's pastoral care for Nouwen was silent and involved no voluntary contact since Adam's disability prevented speaking or reaching out to Nouwen. Nevertheless, Nouwen's life was enriched through his interactions with Adam. Many who have a disability can be actively or passively involved in pastoral care, as was the case with Adam. To dismiss people with a disability as unimportant to the church and not persons with whom we are called to minister, we elevate ourselves as able-bodied persons and create division in the church, which Paul spoke critically about in 1 Corinthians chapters 1 and 3. The danger in dismissing believers with a disability is that nondisabled church leaders and members may end up proclaiming themselves rather than the Lord (cf. 4:5). "Proclaiming self" verbally or attitudinally, is a form of comparative boasting in which Christians with disabilities are deemed not as "important" or "useful" as nondisabled Christians, resulting in an attitude of "smugness" or self-satisfaction: "I'm better than he is," or "I'm so glad I'm not like that person" (oblivious to the fact that being able-bodied may be temporary; disability is only one accident or illness away and often accompanies aging). This self-proclaiming prevents servanthood, to which Christians are called and for which God will hold us accountable.

Since God intentionally chose to work through human weakness to display his glory globally, the apparent weakness of disability is not something shameful or to be hidden. Having this treasure in fragile jars of clay translates into "my weakness plus God's power equals *God's* power ... The power of the gospel comes in our weakness, not in our strength, not in our greatness, but in the fact that we are clay pots – and cracked ones at that!" (Hughes, 2006, p. 94).

Paul wrote that we carry the death of Jesus so that the life of Jesus is manifest in our body because it is God who strengthens us (4:10). This suggests that Christians who have a disability may have an advantage over those who are nondisabled. When Paul says some people are "veiled" from seeing the glory of Christ (4:3), he was referring to unbelievers. But the hearts of believers may also be veiled to seeing the light of the glory of Christ in believers who are disabled, especially if the disability is severe. Some may even think a disabled person is un-savable or has nothing to contribute. Others may believe the person is automatically saved and ignore them evangelistically. Still others may believe the person with a disability is an angel unaware. Scripture does not support any of these thoughts. No one is beyond the gracious, re-creative power of God, and no one is to be excluded from the gospel call.

Barnett (1988) wrote, "The gospel of Christ not only illumines our darkened lives … it transforms them little by little so that they increasingly resemble the moral and spiritual character of the Lord Jesus" (p. 76). Some nondisabled persons cannot (or will not) see this in someone who is disabled, especially if the disability is severe. But as previously said, disability is not more powerful than God. Power in weakness seems contradictory or illogical by human standards, but since revealing Jesus in our lives does not require a fully functional body or mind, a Christian who is disabled but does not surrender to his or her limitations may give a more decisive testimony to the life of Jesus within than a Christian who relies on his own strength.

Paul's words in 4:16–18 aptly apply to people with a disability. Paul says *inwardly,* all Christians are being renewed. That renewal is apprehended by faith and hope. *Outwardly* we all grow weaker and face death. Paul is describing a great exchange that begins when we accept Christ and continues into eternity. Yong (2011) wrote,

> It is more in keeping with Paul's theology of weakness that the more powerful manifestations are mediated through those whose abilities are less noticeable or who are thought to be lesser candidates for God's work from a worldly or 'normal' point of view (p. 94).

The things seen are transient, but the things unseen are eternal (4:18). In 4:17–18, Paul entreated his readers not to lose heart, reminding

David W. Anderson

them that though our outer man, the clay pot, is decaying, the inner man, where the treasure resides, is being renewed daily. The "light affliction" we experience is to our benefit in that it produces an incomparable and eternal weight of glory. Paul's "light and momentary afflictions" included persecution and suffering to the extent that most believers today do not experience, thus giving his words greater weight as we face various issues in this world. "Great though our sense of weakness may be, the power of God is always greater" (Barnett, 1988, p. 32).

EARTHLY TENTS AND GODLY HOPE

For we know that if the tent that is our earthly home is destroyed, we have a building from God, a house not made with hands, eternal in the heavens. For in this tent we groan, longing to put on our heavenly dwelling, if indeed by putting it on we may not be found naked. For while we are still in this tent, we groan, being burdened – not that we would be unclothed, but that we would be further clothed, so that what is mortal may be swallowed up by life. He who has prepared us for this very thing is God, who has given us the Spirit as a guarantee. So we are always of good courage. We know that while we are at home in the body we are away from the Lord, for we walk by faith, not by sight. [8]Yes, we are of good courage, and we would rather be away from the body and at home with the Lord. So whether we are at home or away, we make it our aim to please him. For we must all appear before the judgment seat of Christ, so that each one may receive what is due for what he has done in the body, whether good or evil.

2 Corinthians 5:1-10

"The more people are praising God, the more the world is taking the shape it was meant to have" (Wright, 2004, p. 50). Looking at the shape of the world today suggests that not many are praising God. Many people, focusing solely on the limitations resulting from disability, believe that disability is either a curse or the result of personal or familial sin. They might then ask what such people have to praise God for. Some who birth a child who is disabled, or who become disabled through illness or accident, seek a miraculous cure rather than giving thanks to God in all circumstances (1 Thessalonians 5:18), thereby possibly missing what God wants them to learn about him, grace, and themselves. In Philippians 4:6–7, Paul encouraged rejoicing in the Lord, not being anxious about things, giving thanks, and resting in God's peace. Sometimes it is easier for the person with a disability to rest in God's peace than for someone who is nondisabled but fears the potential outcome of becoming disabled.

In 2 Corinthians 5, Paul speaks of two "ages," one present and one future. The focus of the present age is outward: wrestling with deficiency, disadvantage, disease, disability, and death. The focus of the future age is inward: being renewed by the Spirit of God. Wright (2004) explained that the hope of which Paul spoke is not about "becoming *disembodied* but about being *re-embodied*" (p. 83) – spiritually transformed into the image of Christ (Romans 8:29). Paul juxtaposed our present weakness with our future hope. That the present body is mortal cannot be questioned; we all grow weary, we all die (cf. "Cracked pots," 2 Corinthians 2). However, the future body will be full of life, which nothing can harm, destroy, or disable. But a believer's hope is not simply for the distant future; it is a hope in which we live now, even with our weakness or disability. Paul metaphorically emphasizes the contrast between the inferior, present mode of existence (our earthly and impermanent tent) with God's superior, permanent building (5:1). What we have now is temporal and vulnerable; what we will have in the future is eternal and invulnerable. In a sense, it will be more "real" because it will be as God intended. Grasping this truth enables us to face conflict, pain, disability, and handicaps created by the environment and people's attitudes.

Paul's words are words of promise. But they do not imply that people who live with a physical or intellectual disability are unacceptable, or even that disability itself is unacceptable from God's perspective. This good news is intended to encourage and help us focus on God's blessings here and now and in the future life. Disability is a reminder that we live in a damaged, sin-filled world, that the present world is itself disabled. For a Christian, having a body or mind that is disabled helps them know that God works through our weakness (building on what Paul said earlier regarding weakness and vulnerability, and what he will share in 2 Corinthians 12).

Paul was not promoting denial or withdrawal from reality, but courage and patience as we move through this present life. Our hope as believers is not simply hope for the distant future; it is a present hope, even in our weakness or disability, and it is a living hope, not wishful thinking. We change as the Spirit "grows" us in faith and knowledge of the truth, enabling us to hold to the promise of 5:1 that, though everything is destroyed (including our own death), our eternal home in heaven remains. Paul acknowledged that God is in charge, working all things together for good for those called according to his purpose (Romans 8:28). Neither death nor disability can deprive us of the glory of the coming age. Whom God has called, he also justified; whom he has justified will be glorified (Romans 8:30). Disability does not deprive us of anything of true and lasting value. Christians whose disability limits them in some way may have a greater degree of hope than Christians who are nondisabled, perhaps even a greater blessing because of bringing glory to God in their present state.

Believers with a disability don't waste time dreaming about becoming un-disabled, in this world or the next, because their faith is in God and his ability to carry them through any trials or difficulties stemming from their disability. They are confident that God is at work to transform them spiritually and certain that God can and will use them for his glory. A cure is not necessary. It is those without a disability, including Christians and church leaders, who seem to question God's ability to work in and through people who are disabled. Both able-bodied and disabled have been saved and equipped through the Holy Spirit to serve the Lord and others in his name. Being justified through faith has brought us peace with God (Romans 5:1) and peace with disability. Our salvation is not *because* of good works we have done, but so that we *can do* good the works God has planned for us and planned us for (Ephesians 2:8–10).

Nothing about disability prohibits a life of serving the Lord and serving others in his name. We need a broad understanding of what serving means. We quickly see "religious" activity (preaching, teaching, singing, leading worship, etc.) as serving. But arranging the room for worship, handing out worship folders, and cleaning up afterward are things which can be done even by someone who is intellectually challenged – quite possibly done more meticulously and joyfully than able-bodied folks, and with no expectation of earthly (financial) reward. In 1 Corinthians 10:31, Paul wrote that whatever we do is to be done to the glory of God. "Whatever" leaves room for a lot of activity not requiring an able body or mind. What matters is faith working through love (Galatians 5:6). In Ephesians 2:10, Paul wrote that we are God's workmanship, created in Christ Jesus for good works, which God prepared beforehand. "We" is all-inclusive, disabled and able-bodied alike.

All earthly ministry is ultimately God's work, and all Christians are ministers. Shults and Sandage (2006) wrote, "To be a Christian is to be 'in' ministry – to be ministering to (serving) others, which is how the Spirit of love is manifested in the community for the 'common good'" (p. 120). God can work in us and through us despite our weakness or disability – perhaps even more effectively in people who have a disability because they recognize God's strength and gifting working through them. Being able-bodied can get in the way of God's work if trust is placed solely in personal ability and power rather than in God. Our being disabled does not "handicap" God, limiting his ability to accomplish his will. Hope for the future is a powerful motivation, but hope for a disabled believer is not hope in a "cure." It is a restful hope that God will be glorified and that they will spend eternity with Jesus.

Paul says in 5:2, "while we are still in this tent, we groan, longing to put on our heavenly dwelling." This "groaning" is not literal, like the complaining we might do when things do not go as we hoped or when we experience physical pain. Nor does "groaning" refer to a death wish because of being physically or intellectually disabled. Rather, it is a groaning of anticipation. "Paul's groaning was a gift from God" (Hughes, 2006, p. 106) tied to the guarantee that God is transforming us now and the promise of ultimate and complete transformation. Paul's confidence is expressed in 5:5–7, where he spoke of walking by faith, not by sight. This connects to what Paul wrote in 4:17–18 about our light and momentary affliction preparing for us an eternal weight of glory beyond all comparison, and not looking to temporary things, but things unseen and eternal. For some, "momentary affliction" may include disability, which is not eternal. Pleasing God and bringing him glory is what is important to Paul (5:9). It should be our desire as well. Paul said, "whether we are at home or away, we make it our aim to please God." Whether able-bodied or disabled, our goal is the same.

The change in Paul's metaphor in 5:1ff – from *tent* to *building* – and the hope embodied in this imagery is relevant to disability because its focus is on present hope and future fulfillment. In Philippians 3:30–31, Paul spoke of Jesus transforming our lowly body to be like Christ's glorious body. In 1 Corinthians 15: 50–53, he wrote about our perishable bodies putting on the imperishable, our mortal body putting on immortality. This change is something that all Christians eagerly await. The sure hope (not wishful thinking) of change for a Christian who is disabled may be a purer hope than that of nondisabled Christians in that it is not focused solely on physical renewal. Browne (1997) asked,

> May not the presence of imperfection be a vibrant indication that something more, something radically transcendent to finite natures, lies just beyond? Can't we see that this apparent design aberration [disability] does not deflect God's beauty, God's ineffable perfection, but simply evidences our lack of imagination, our limited finite capabilities? (p. 35)

In 5:1–10, Paul gives three fundamental principles: walk by faith, not by sight (5:7), always be of good courage (5:6 and 5:8), and aim to please Christ (5:9). *"Walking by faith"* for those who are physically disabled can include crawling or wheeling or being pushed on a gurney, or using a cane or being led by a sighted guide for those who are visually impaired. Living by sight is acting as if we are in control of things and relying on our ability or supposed importance (Millar, 2020) rather than cleaving, by faith, to the knowledge that only things of the Lord will last. Able-bodied folks tend to trust in their own ability, strength, or knowledge. People who have a disability acknowledge their weakness and trust that God can work in and through them as they draw on his strength. They know that the glory goes to God, not to self. *"To be of good courage"* (5:6, 8) accompanies walking by faith and draws on a personal relationship or identification with the Lord so that whatever we do is done in the name of the Lord (Colossians 3:17). *"Pleasing Christ"* (5:9) begins with living by faith, stressing a personal relationship with the Lord, and Jesus's living in and through us. Faith, courage, and pleasing Christ undergird the believer's hope: the confident expectation that God will do all that he has promised.

Courtney (2011) described the gospel message as one of hope amid despair and suffering, revealing God's love and actions on behalf of his creatures, but not necessarily in ways we expect or desire. God *could* miraculously alter a genetic condition that leads to disability, but we waste our time praying and waiting for that to happen. Having Christ at our side does not necessitate the removal of a disability. Instead, we should seek God's wisdom and "cure" for our attitude and allow him to use believers in their weakness or disability for his glory. It is not about us; it is about him. Our plans and desires may never come to fruition, but God never fails. The Bible often speaks about God's using human weakness to bring glory to himself – Moses's speech difficulty and Gideon's assumed weakness, for example. Paul's life and teaching is a strong example of disability rightly viewed and rightly used.

Western cultural ideals show a clear bias toward physical perfection and attractiveness, resulting in fear of limitation or loss of ability. Disability is seen as "deviance," which suggests that happiness is unavailable to persons with a disability from an ablest viewpoint. Paul counters this by stressing contentment rather than worldly happiness (Philippians 4:4–8). Knowing that God is with us even in the midst of struggles or disabilities brings encouragement and hope. Our disability does not negate God's sovereignty, wisdom, love, and grace, nor is God's goodness challenged if he does not intervene to prevent or cure a disabling condition.

Our attitude is often our greatest disability, preventing us from seeing *possibility*. "With God all things are possible" (Matthew 19:26); our disability does not handicap God. Even severe mental or physical limitations are no obstacle to God, nor do they indicate God's judgment – or God's absence – in a person's life.

For believers, Jesus is our identity, not disability, and we are being conformed to his image (Romans 8:29). To be designated "disabled" says nothing about who the person is or what he or she may be capable of doing (in fact, medical and psychological labels often fail to tell us much about what the person *cannot* do). A disability does not prevent a Christian from demonstrating joy and contentment nor limit the ability to bring blessing to others. Even a severe physical impairment and inability to speak (such as with Adam, Elliot, and Soila) do not affect the ability to express love and peace to others.

Rather than center on the disability, we need to focus on God, who can communicate his love to us even through people with a disability (cf. Nouwen's "Adam, 1997). Paul's exhortation is to focus on things worthy of praise (Philippians 4:8). Thinking about God's goodness, contemplating his love and presence in our lives and in the lives of Christians who deal with physical or intellectual limitations, can alter how we view disability and allow us to see ways we or our disabled loved one can bring joy and blessing to others, and bring glory to God – perhaps even to praise God for disability.

GOD-CENTERED RELATIONSHIPS

We walk by faith, not by sight … For the love of Christ controls us, because we have concluded this: that one has died for all, therefore all have died; and he died for all, that those who live might no longer live for themselves but for him who for their sake died and was raised. From now on, therefore, we regard no one according to the flesh. Even though we once regarded Christ according to the flesh, we regard him thus no longer. Therefore, if anyone is in Christ, he is a new creation. The old has passed away; behold, the new has come. All this is from God, who through Christ reconciled us to himself and gave us the ministry of reconciliation; that is, in Christ God was reconciling the world to himself, not counting their trespasses against them, and entrusting to us the message of reconciliation. Therefore, we are ambassadors for Christ, God making his appeal through us. We implore you on behalf of Christ, be reconciled to God. For our sake he made him to be sin who knew no sin, so that in him we might become the righteousness of God.

2 Corinthians 5:7, 14–21

Zack Eswine (2014) wrote in his commentary on Ecclesiastes, "our whole purpose as human beings is a God-centered relationship toward all things" (p. 17). Though evil and discord in our world are apparent, and we long for the new heavens and new earth (2 Peter 3:13), we are even now to display God-centered relationships. Having a God-centered relationship toward all things includes all people, even those with a disability. In this passage from 2 Corinthians, Paul declared that we are a new creation and must no longer regard people from a worldly perspective. God has reconciled us to Himself through Christ, not counting our sins against us. We rest in this truth. Paul continued this thought by saying God has given us the ministry of reconciliation (5:18).

In the epistle to the Galatians, Paul said we live in Christ as Christ lives in us. Our "walk" as Christians must therefore accord with the earthly life of Jesus. This necessitates rejecting cultural stereotypes regarding disability and people who have a disability, not regarding them according to the flesh (5:16). Paul's statement that we walk by faith, not by sight (5:7) applies to how we view and treat people different from the norm. The ministry of Jesus was counter-cultural, evidenced by Jesus's attention to widows, orphans, children, and people with a disability rather than catering to the religious elite. Though Jesus was criticized for spending time with "sinners" (cf. Matthew 9:10–13; Luke 5:31–32; Luke 15:1–2), his mission was to announce and embody good news to the poor, liberty to the captives, recovery of sight to the blind, liberty to the oppressed, and to proclaim the year of the Lord's favor (Luke 4:18–19). Jesus's parting words to his disciples (Matthew 28:18–20) make this our mission, too.

The Bible says all humankind is created in (or as) God's image, including those born with a disability, thereby affirming the intrinsic worth of each person. Their accomplishments or their disabilities do not define people. In Psalm 139:13–16, David detailed God's involvement in the creation of every individual, knitting us together according to his design, including our physicality as well as our abilities. Personal differences, including strengths, weaknesses, and disabilities, are part of his design and part of the vast diversity of God's creation.

Individuals and families affected by disability worldwide constitute one of the largest overlooked people groups in the world (an estimated 15% of the world's population). In many countries, they are also among the poorest. A worldly, elitist view of this people group is often more handicapping than the disability itself and contributes to ongoing injustice and prejudice on the part of the nondisabled. This elitist view may be as or more confining than the actual physical, emotional, or intellectual disability itself.

In Galatians 3:28, Paul wrote, "There is neither Jew nor Greek, there is neither slave nor free, there is no male and female, for you are all one in Christ Jesus." We can extend this list to include there being no artificial separation between disabled and able-bodied. Actions that accord with Paul's words will enable the church of Christ to become a church without barriers and evidence a practical theology of inclusion. Jesus's warning about placing a stumbling block before "little ones" who believe in him (Matthew 18:6) includes not putting a stumbling block before people who have a disability. Churches must reach out to individuals and families with disability in love.

Paul explained that anyone in Christ is a new creation – the old has passed away, and the new has come (5:17). This spiritual re-creation leads to seeing things and people with different eyes, eyes that the Spirit of God has opened. Having eyes of faith impacts how we interpret and react to our experiences and how we see our role as ambassadors of Christ and see possibilities in others. It means seeing things and seeing people with disabilities as God does.

And it means not living for ourselves, but for Christ (5:15). Living for self and people "like us," failing to extend love and the gospel to people and families affected by disability, fails to obey Christ's instruction to reach all people groups with the good news of the gospel. It presents the church, if not Jesus himself, as being prejudiced in who is "eligible" to receive Christ in faith and who Jesus has sent us to as his ambassadors.

Stott (1992) wrote about holistic ministry and the relationship between evangelism and social responsibility and warned about separating one from the other. To emphasize the relationship of words and actions, he wrote:

> [W]ords remain abstract until they are made concrete in deeds of love, while works remain ambiguous until they are interpreted by the proclamation of the gospel. Words without works lack credibility; works without words lack clarity. So Jesus's works made his words visible; his words made his works intelligible (p. 345).

In the context of ministry to and with persons with a disability, a broader polarization remains in that we agree with Paul that Christ died for all and commanded us to take the good news to all people groups (Matthew 28:18–20), but many Christians and churches have allowed an exception to Jesus's command by ignoring (by oversight or choice) individuals and families impacted by disability. Polarization results from believing that the degree of disability places a person beyond the reach of the gospel or from the incorrect assumption that the disability is the result of personal sin, making the sin or the person "unforgivable." Some churches believe that God cannot accept, reside in, or use a person who is disabled and conclude the person has insufficient faith and send them away. Though their words say "God so loved the world," their actions limit who God's love and grace can be extended to, thereby limiting God.

Failure to extend (and to live) the gospel to people whom society, the world, or the church rejects demonstrates a judgment that they are unworthy of time and effort. This reflects a prideful attitude, using human standards to determine who God can redeem. In this way, we put ourselves in God's place and add a qualification as to who can become part of God's family. Thus, we limit the scope of Christ's redemption.

Connor (2012) suggested that acting in this manner amounts to saying that living with a disability is an unacceptable way of being human or at least an unacceptable way of being a Christian. This might be the conclusion perceptive people, disabled or nondisabled, make when looking at many churches and noting the absence of persons with apparent disabilities and the lack of any form of ministry oriented toward people and families dealing with disability. Noting this overt prejudice, some of these families may leave the church or reject the gospel entirely. The church, then, creates spiritual nomads. Churches should be places where people with disabilities develop social relationships, come to understand themselves beyond a medical diagnosis and gain a sense of belonging and connectedness. "This sense of validation and belonging mitigates the hopelessness of loneliness" (Connor, 2012, p. 32).

God calls both nondisabled and disabled believers into a relationship with him and with others in the body of Christ. The presence of God and grace in each believer colors that relationship and is based on love, not charity or paternalism. The goal is not simply to include persons and families affected by disability but also for them to gain a sense of belonging. The attitude of church leaders and the laity are critical in creating this atmosphere of acceptance and caring. What works against this is that many nondisabled people "boast" in their ability and contribution to the church, potentially setting themselves above those who are disabled.

Paul spoke of love as a controlling factor in the life of a believer (5:14). This calls for a response to others characterized by love for God and one another. To say, as did Paul, that Christ died for *all* is an inclusive

David W. Anderson

statement. But in the heart of some believers, "all" is restricted to persons who are nondisabled. Being controlled by love extends to our motivation, words, and actions toward God and toward others.

Phillips' (2004) book, "Your God is Too Small," may describe churches and Christians who fail to reach out to persons dealing with disability, welcoming them as an important part of the fellowship. The Bible is clear that God is big enough to include people with disabilities in his kingdom. It is not God who is small, but the heart of some Christians is too small when it comes to reaching out to people with disabilities. Paul said Christians no longer live for themselves (5:15) nor regard others according to the flesh (5:16). To not look on others according to the flesh means not seeing someone as a *disabled* person, with all the negativity and prejudice that entails, but simply as a *person* who has a disability. Because Paul regarded no one according to the flesh, he could see the least likely of converts as having immense potential (Hughes, 2006). Because people with a significant disability are often viewed negatively, their potential goes unnoticed and untapped.

Millar (2020) wrote, "loving as Christ did is at the core of authentic Christian ministry … if our grasp of the gospel increases, then so will our love for other people" (pp. 88–89). The authentic gospel message is good news that applies to all people, nondisabled and disabled alike. It is a deeply theological message but also profoundly relational and should result in significant differences in how people and families dealing with disability are seen.

By virtue of our new creation, Paul said the old is gone, and the new has come (5:16–17): we no longer live for self and we do not regard Christ from a worldly perspective. Love becomes our compelling motivation; selfishness is gone. Difficulties, hardships, and disability (actual and potential) are not removed, but our faith in Christ removes fear – of disability and of people who are disabled.

RECONCILIATION

Therefore, knowing the fear of the Lord, we persuade others. But
what we are is known to God, and I hope it is known also to your
conscience … For the love of Christ controls us, because we have
concluded this: that one has died for all, therefore all have died; and
he died for all, that those who live might no longer live for themselves
but for him who for their sake died and was raised. From now on,
therefore, we regard no one according to the flesh. Even though we
once regarded Christ according to the flesh, we regard him thus no
longer. Therefore, if anyone is in Christ, he is a new creation. The old
has passed away; behold, the new has come. All this is from God,
who through Christ reconciled us to himself and gave us the ministry
of reconciliation; that is, in Christ God was reconciling the world to
himself, not counting their trespasses against them, and entrusting to us
the message of reconciliation. Therefore, we are ambassadors for Christ,
God making his appeal through us. We implore you on behalf of Christ,
be reconciled to God. For our sake he made him to be sin who knew
no sin, so that in him we might become the righteousness of God.

2 Corinthians 5:11, 14–21

"Looking at disability as something to be repaired is almost exclusively
a nondisabled person's point of view" (Morstad, 2018, p. 6). For people
born with or who acquire a disability at an early age, living with disability
is "normal." But for nondisabled persons, the possibility of becoming
disabled can create anxiety about what they might "lose," how they would
cope, and what impact it would have on their family. Lacking a proper
understanding of disability, and absent prior experience with a disabled
person often leads to avoidance of people who are disabled, especially if
the disability is severe. Parents of young nondisabled children may usher

them away from children or adults who are disabled, sending an unvoiced message that such people should be avoided. Attributing disability to sin, God's punishment, or shallow faith leads some to conclude it best not to interact with severely disabled persons, disregarding Jesus's commands to carry the gospel to every people group (Matthew 28:18–20) and to love our neighbors as we love ourselves (Matthew 5:44, 22:39).

Devotion to the Lord undergirds Paul's ministry. The New Living Translation of 5:11 clearly expresses his motivation: "Because we understand our fearful responsibility to the Lord, we work hard to persuade others. God knows we are sincere." Zealously proclaiming the gospel is Paul's response to God's love which now "controls him" (5:14). Given the absence of church ministry to and with persons who are disabled, I have to wonder if many Christians do not fear (love) the Lord enough to share the gospel with disabled persons. Does fear of interacting with individuals with severe impairments, or the assumption that they will be unable to understand the gospel, outweigh the need to obey Jesus's command to "go into all the world and proclaim the gospel to the whole creation" (Mark 16:15)? Paul asserts that all have sinned and fallen short of the glory of God (Romans 3:13) but that Christ has died for all (5:14). *All* is an inclusive word, encompassing people of all physical and intellectual ability levels. But how can they believe unless someone shares the gospel with them, verbally or through actions (Romans 10:13–15)?

The main thrust of 2 Corinthians 5 is reconciliation, which MacArthur (2003) described as being at the heart of Paul's preaching (cf. Romans 5:10–11, Colossians 1:20–22, and Ephesians 2:13–16). The reconciliation Paul spoke of is not the result of God calling sinners to join him at the table to hammer out an agreement. Biblical reconciliation flows solely from the grace of God, whereby God's enmity toward humankind is removed (Nicole, 2002). Thus, reconciliation is the cornerstone of Christ's atoning work. Enmity between God and man is removed as Christ's righteousness is exchanged for our sin, enabling a new relationship with God through Christ. In Colossians 1:19–22, Paul described the process and intent of reconciliation more fully:

> For in (Christ) all the fullness of God was pleased to dwell, and through him to reconcile to himself all things,

whether on earth or in heaven, making peace by the blood of his cross. And you, who once were alienated and hostile in mind, doing evil deeds, he has now reconciled in his body of flesh by his death, in order to present you holy and blameless and above reproach before him.

Reconciliation is based on the saving work of Christ, which stems from God's loving heart. It is a gift of God's grace, not a reward for something we have done or a situation we have endured. Reconciliation is something we simply embrace (MacArthur, 2003). The "all things" God has reconciled to himself includes disability, but this neither means nor requires removing a person's disability in this life. To be reconciled yet remain disabled does not indicate a lack of love or care on God's part, nor does it suggest that God is unable to save a person who is disabled. Reconciliation with disability means no longer seeing it as something to be feared; disability is not anti-God. God can bring glory to himself and blessing to others through a person who has a disability (as in the international ministries of Joni Eareckson Tada and Cordell Brown, or individuals like Elliot, Soila, and Adam, previously mentioned).

Reconciliation deals with attitudes of the heart, acceptance, and trust. Paul's focus is not solely on our standing with God; he also spoke of reconciliation's impact on how we relate to others (5:16). Christians have been given both the ministry and the message of reconciliation (5:18–19). "Ministry" and "message" are relatively synonymous and refer to *proclaiming* the message and *living* the message: embodying reconciliation in our lifestyle and interactions with others. "Message" refers to the good news that through Christ, believers are adopted into God's family. This "is a message we need to speak *and* live out" (Millar, 2020, p. 91, emphasis added), making it necessary that we cultivate authentic, loving relationships with others, marked by forgiveness and genuine friendships, and making God's reconciling power apparent in our lives. This has clear implications for ministering to and with individuals and families affected by disability. In taking the first step toward reconciliation with people who have a disability, Christians reflect the character of God, who did not wait for us to seek him, but came seeking us (cf. Venske, 2018). The ministry and message of reconciliation involve both proclaiming the good news verbally and doing good works. Demonstrating the gospel through good works often has a more significant impact than a well-structured sermon.

"Ministry" does not simply refer to being a pastor or serving as a missionary; it is a task in which all believers are to engage. The church seeks to equip its members, both able-bodied and disabled, for ministry. This equipping begins with expecting every believer, able-bodied and disabled, to have at least one spiritual gift, and helping them identify, develop, and use their gifts in the church and the world. The list of gifts mentioned by Paul in 1 Corinthians 12 is not exhaustive, and how they are defined and manifested must not be limited by our presumptions. Defining the gifts too narrowly leads even some nondisabled believers to think the Spirit passed them by in the distribution or to regard physically or intellectually impaired believers as "too disabled" to be of any use. Disability does not limit God's desire and ability to work in and through a person to bring spiritual blessing and growth to that person and to others through that person.

Our commission as Christians is to proclaim the gospel and display actions consistent with the message, following Jesus's model. Jesus's mission statement in Luke 4:18-19 provides a general guide to our ministry and message of reconciliation:

> The Spirit of the Lord is upon me, because he has anointed
> me to proclaim good news to the poor. He has sent me
> to proclaim liberty to the captives and recovering of sight
> to the blind, to set at liberty those who are oppressed, to
> proclaim the year of the Lord's favor.

We cannot perform miracles, but our lives and words can give visual proof of how Jesus has changed our lives as we interact with others. Jesus's ability to change lives is not limited just to the lives of nondisabled people.

Reconciliation with God and others is foundational to the Christian faith, making the need to demonstrate this theological truth in our actions paramount. God committed to us the *message* of reconciliation (5:19), and commissioned us to engage in a *ministry* of reconciliation (5:18), calling others to be reconciled with God (Colossians 1:21–22; Romans

5:10), with others (Ephesians 2:16), and with themself as a new creation (2 Corinthians 5:17).

Paul connected the human-body/church-body analogy (introduced in 1 Corinthians 12) to reconciliation: "In reconciling all things to himself, God forms us into one body in Christ. It is only as we are joined to the body of Christ that we are reconciled to God" (Parrett & Kang, 2009, p. 33). This also emphasizes reconciliation *among* believers. Just as the parts of our physical body work in unity, so must the church function as "one." The parts of our physical body do not function apart from the head or act independently of other parts. Legs that don't work because of paralysis or minds limited because of Down syndrome are nonetheless part of the physical body.

Similarly, being reconciled to Christ necessitates interconnection among the different parts of the body of Christ, including unity among nondisabled and disabled members. Believers who have physical or intellectual disabilities remain essential parts of the body of Christ, opening us to relationships not based on familiarity or sameness but on our oneness in Christ. How we treat, speak with (or about) these "weaker" parts of the church body must communicate love and respect, not pity, hesitation, or patronization.

Our commission to take the gospel to *every* people group includes sharing the message with people who have a disability. Unity and fellowship with people who are disabled provide the opportunity to serve others as Christ did and help us recognize our own weaknesses. Failure to include people with a disability as valued and valuable parts of the body is to question God's love and represents the church as a fragmented and dysfunctional body (Parrett & Kang, 2009). Embodying the ministry and message of reconciliation and including people with disabilities allows the church to reflect the character of God "as individuals are established in their identity in Christ, as the body of Christ grows together relationally, and as individuals and congregations focus outward in service and mission" (Venzke, 2018, p. 36). Parrett and Kang (2009) wrote, "There can be no vision of being reconciled to God that does not include being reconciled to one another in and through the church" (p. 35). Because a person has a severe disability does not negate sharing with them the ministry or message of reconciliation. And Christians with severe disabilities are not excused from the task of sharing with others the ministry and message of reconciliation, though how they share may be different.

Biblical reconciliation involves a radical transformation of relationships from enmity to friendship and harmony with God and others (Anderson, 2013). Biblical teaching about living and loving, about being in a relationship with God and others, and about sin, grace, and forgiveness inform our ministry and message of reconciliation. Churches must help nondisabled members accept and appreciate those who are disabled and enable both groups to realize their strengths and abilities and develop their God-given potential, sometimes in creative ways.

Paul wrote, "There is neither Jew nor Greek, there is neither slave nor free, there is no male and female, for [we] are all one in Christ Jesus" (Galatians 3:28). We can add to Paul's thought that there is no distinction between disabled and able-bodied. Having an able body or mind does not make one a better person (or a better Christian); God shows no favoritism or partiality (Acts 10:34, Romans 2:11). James 2:1–9 ties impartiality to loving our neighbors as we love ourselves. Paul called for devotion to and honoring of one another out of genuine love (Romans 12:9–10), doing nothing out of selfish ambition but counting others as more significant than ourselves (Philippians 2:3–4) – including people with severe disabilities. We are to seek the good of our neighbors (1 Corinthians 12:24) and bear one another's burdens (Galatians 6:2). Such practical actions demonstrate love, promote reconciliation with others, and are especially needful and meaningful when interacting with someone with a severe intellectual or physical disability. Looking to the interest of others demonstrates the same mindset as Jesus, who came not to be served but to serve (Matthew 20:28).

Jesus's ministry embraced people who were disabled. His compassion for the harassed and helpless people marginalized by society (Matthew 9:36), his parable of the Great Banquet (Luke 14:15–24), and his identifying himself with the least of his "brothers" (Matthew 25:31–46), all connect to the ministry and message of reconciliation to which God has called every believer. But despite Jesus's and Paul's clear teaching, few churches actively reach out to individuals and families dealing with disability or welcome them into the fellowship. Many disabled persons feel they are "dis-invited" by churches (Webb-Mitchell, 1994).

In Ephesians 2:13–16, Paul described Christians as once being far off but now brought near in Christ, God having taken away the barrier of hostility between Jews and Gentiles and making believers from each group one in Christ. In the same way, God has removed the humanly erected barrier resulting from how the majority population views people with disabilities. From a worldly perspective, people's worth is based on what they have or can accomplish. People with even a mild disability are often presumed to be dependent on others and able to accomplish little of what the world deems important. Thus, they may be ignored or stigmatized, seen as having no intrinsic worth or dignity as individuals created in God's image. God has broken down this "wall of separation," but many churches have not. God's love is perfect and unconditional. We are all uniquely created and loved by God. God does not bring us into his family because of our strength, ability, or intelligence (which are from God in the first place). God simply wants our love, fellowship, and worship, none of which require a certain level of physical or intellectual ability. Believers, disabled and nondisabled alike, belong to God purely by his grace (cf. Ephesians 2:8–10). God can and does work in and through believers, even in their weakness or disability, because then God's power is on display (2 Corinthians 12).

Until getting to know the person who is disabled, many think of themselves more highly than they should, which Paul warned against in Romans 12:3, thus, we are self-deceived (Galatians 6:3). Judging people by their appearance feeds the myth that disabled persons have nothing to offer or are more limited than they genuinely are. Our attention should be on the person, not the disability. As we develop a relationship with that person, the disability "disappears," and we are able to see the beauty of the person, and through that relationship, to see how disability can be a blessing (cf. 2 Corinthians 12). "People with disabilities allow believers the opportunity to demonstrate love for God, love for people, and faithfulness" (Deuel, 2013, p. 88). At the same time, they are models for nondisabled Christians on how to live a loving and faithful life, especially under challenging circumstances.

Reconciliation with others involves counting them as more significant than ourselves and looking to their interests (Philippians 2:3–4). Is merely allowing them into the worship center sufficient? Connor (2012) wrote of "place-sharing," a form of affirming presence (p. 45), as intentional friendships with the individual and the family impacted by disability are established. Being present, sharing life, not just space, is more important than "doing for" them (which we sometimes assume is necessary but can be disrespectful). The ministry of presence fosters reconciliation. And as genuine friendships are formed, ministry becomes bi-directional: those with a disability minister to us even as we minister to them. Ministry centers on positive actions of sharing or shouldering burdens, helping our friends stand strong despite the limitations of disability, thereby fulfilling the law of Christ (Galatians 6:2, John 13:34–35), and showing ourselves to be Jesus's disciples. Through loving care, we serve one another (Galatians 5:13). "By reconciling nondisabled and disabled people, the church can be transformed into an inclusive fellowship where strangers of any type … and anyone who is feeling estrangement, can experience belonging and embrace" (Hoeksema, 2009, p. 37).

Paul said, "from now on we regard no one according to the flesh" (5:16). This allows us to see disabled persons, not as the weakest of Christians, but as Christians with great potential when in the hands of God. "Potential" is not limited to impressive preaching, musical talent, or powerful praying. Adam, the young disabled adult with whom Nouwen (1997) worked, had severe limitations, yet still reflected the love of God and blessed those who took the time to know him. Soila and Elliot readily employ their spiritual gifts in worship and service, drawing others into deeper worship. But rather than reaching out to the Adams, Elliots, and Soilas with grace-filled love and a servant's heart, many Christians turn away, missing the opportunity to "be" Christ to them and *see* Christ in them, thereby receiving the gift and blessing they offer.

When Paul spoke of not regarding others based on outward appearance (5:12) or from a worldly perspective (5:16), it is unlikely he had in mind people with a disability, but his words apply to our thinking about disability. A "worldly" view focuses on outward appearance, seeing people, especially those with severe or profound disabilities, as damaged goods, lacking value, and a drain on society, family, or church. Instead, we need to see them through the eyes of grace. Both nondisabled and disabled persons are equally in need of God's grace and, in responding positively to the gospel message, become new creations.

One practical outcome of reconciled attitudes toward individuals and families who deal with disability is reducing their feeling of isolation. Wolfe and Spangler (2018) emphasized the need for a place where these individuals and families will be embraced and can embrace others. The church should be a place where everyone is welcome regardless of ability or other differences. Part of loving and serving people with disabilities is removing roadblocks to relationships and belonging, such as isolation and injustice, barriers built from attitudes of superiority of able-bodied persons who equate disability with weakness, limitation, abnormality, deviance, or dysfunction. Viewing them as inferior and less worthy continues their marginalization. But segregating disabled persons also isolates the nondisabled, reinforcing their false sense of superiority. Only God is superior. A feeling of superiority among nondisabled persons interferes with the ministry and message of reconciliation and constitutes a denial of the full humanity of disabled persons. The presumption that people with a disability are in need of pity or charity, ignoring strengths they may have, disregards the biblical teaching that all people are created in God's image. Some churches have developed a disability ministry and may have a pastor or elder whose specific focus is individuals and families who deal with disability. This is a positive step, but "ministry" is something *all* Christians are called to, not just those professionally trained. Limited physical or intellectual ability does not determine who ministers and who is ministered to. Spiritual gifting is not related to cognitive or physical prowess. Since Christians are one body, we need all the body parts to be involved as God enables. Relationship with is more critical than ministry to.

The thought that people with disabilities (even severe) have nothing to teach "us" but are simply in need leads to attitudes of self-promotion, creating divisions in the church (a problem which Paul has previously addressed). As a result, certain parts of the church body may be ignored or under-served, and the church fails to love God and our neighbors as we love ourselves, an attitude that results in our loss and tarnishes the image and message of Christ.

All Christians are purposed to be God's agents of grace to others, regardless of ability or disability. Bredin (2007) argued that Christians must be alert to or create possibilities for relating to people with profound disabilities because "such personal relationships open them to the beauty of divine grace" (p. 4). Feelings of self-sufficiency or autonomy can cause us to miss God's grace or to withhold God's grace from people that are deemed unworthy. People with disabilities grace us by helping us recognize our limitations, challenging our assumption of self-sufficiency, and raising our awareness that we may not be as healthy and capable as we think. Developing a genuine friendship with someone with a disability allows a better understanding of the dynamic nature of grace rather than merely "resting" in the grace that has reconciled us to God.

Wolfe and Spangler (2018) suggested God may be able to minister more powerfully through persons who are disabled than through the nondisabled people because they may be willing to minister in ways nondisabled individuals feel are beneath them, perhaps joyfully serving in more menial capacities. God often accomplishes greater things through what many perceive as weakness than through the self-focused strengths of others.

Some Christians may not fully comprehend grace or understand it to refer only to their salvation. Some may assume a person with a severe disability cannot be loved or graced by God because they cannot "do." But God's grace is not something we earn, nor does it require a certain level of "performance-ability." Believers with a disability, whether mild or severe, often model a more appropriate response to God because they understand their limitations, whereas nondisabled Christians may rest in their self-perceived strengths. But a Christian's hope is not in what we accomplish in our own strength. The psalmist wrote, "the LORD takes pleasure in those who fear [honor, worship, reverence] him, in those whose hope is in his steadfast [constant] love" (Psalm 147:11). Our "doing" is restricted to honoring and reverencing God, not earning God's favor by our works. Anything we accomplish is based on God's gifting and enabling, not something achieved on our own.

The ministry and message of reconciliation also address reconciliation with ourselves, laying aside thoughts of self-importance or self-depreciation. We acknowledge our sins, praise God for his love and forgiveness, and humbly offer into his service "who" and "what" we are, including our abilities or disabilities, knowing that we are valued and loved by God just as we are. Despite our "weakness" – or even *through* our weakness – we serve and glorify God. Better to have a "weak" body or mind but have God in our heart than to be strong-bodied but enter eternity without Christ.

For the person who is disabled, reconciliation with self involves "owning" that disability: acknowledging it as part of who they are, including it in their "story," and choosing to move forward with the disability rather than denying or refusing to go on at all (Langer, 2011). They are, and have, much more than a disability.

Paul said Christians are ambassadors of Christ (5:20). This is true of both nondisabled and disabled Christians. Bennett (1998) pointed out that the word translated "ambassadors" is actually a verb, referring to the Christian's role as a representative of Christ and speaking for him. This applies to all believers, not just those in a leadership position and not just those considered "normal" by the world's standards. Being an ambassador can take many forms – from Paul to Billy Graham, to Cordell Brown, to Joni Eareckson Tada, to Soila, to Elliot. Ambassadors do not speak on their own behalf but represent the one who sent them. Paul declared that his behavior and character were evidence of the truth and authority of his ministry. If the church ignores individuals and families dealing with issues of disability, can the same be said of us? As an ambassador of Christ, our role is crucial as we interact with or relate to individuals and families dealing with disability. As Christ's ambassadors, what we do (or fail to do) reflects on Jesus. The gospel accounts of Jesus's ministry and interactions with people who were disabled or cast aside by the religious elite provides a model for how we are to interact with them: with love and grace and acceptance (cf. Jesus's teaching in the parable of the great banquet in Luke 14:12–24).

Being controlled by the love of Christ (5:14) speaks to our motivation and the direction our lives should take, constraining and compelling us to reach out to others, especially those rejected or despised by the world. Being ourselves "new creations" (5:17) gives us a different way of looking at disability and people with disabilities. Having been given the ministry and the message of reconciliation causes us to reflect on what we say and what we do as Christ's ambassadors. Jesus *embodied* reconciliation; so must we. We must reflect on what practical things being an ambassador for Christ entails, especially concerning individuals and families affected by disability.

There is, then, an "inward" and an "outward" aspect to reconciliation. The inward aspect is God's reconciling us and bringing us into a new relationship with him as part of the body of Christ. Outward reconciliation deals with our relationship with others, including individuals and families who struggle with disability itself. Thus we no longer regard people "according to" to the flesh (5:16). We recognize and respect the limitations resulting from physical or intellectual disability, but we understand that the *person* is not "a disability." We do not judge them as the world does; they are not "poor unfortunates" to be cast aside, kept out of sight, or terminated through abortion or denial of medical care. Outward reconciliation allows us to recognize that people with a disability are also created as God's image, giving them value regardless of the degree of disability. Outward reconciliation necessitates discarding prejudicial and discriminatory thoughts about people who have a disability, and welcoming them into the church fellowship.

SOWING AND REAPING, ABOUNDING, AND THANKSGIVING

The point is this: whoever sows sparingly will also reap sparingly, and whoever sows bountifully will also reap bountifully. Each one must give as he has decided in his heart, not reluctantly or under compulsion, for God loves a cheerful giver. And God is able to make all grace abound to you, so that having all sufficiency in all things at all times, you may abound in every good work. As it is written, "He has distributed freely, he has given to the poor; his righteousness endures forever." He who supplies seed to the sower and bread for food will supply and multiply your seed for sowing and increase the harvest of your righteousness. You will be enriched in every way to be generous in every way, which through us will produce thanksgiving to God.

For the ministry of this service is not only supplying the needs of the saints but is also overflowing in many thanksgivings to God. By their approval of this service, they will glorify God because of your submission that comes from your confession of the gospel of Christ, and the generosity of your contribution for them and for all others, while they long for you and pray for you, because of the surpassing grace of God upon you. Thanks be to God for his inexpressible gift!

2 Corinthians 9:6–15

Chapters 8 and 9 of 2 Corinthians are essentially "a call to be open-hearted, wholehearted, gospel-hearted followers of Jesus" (Millar, 2020, p. 125). Though Paul dealt specifically with financial giving and generosity, what he presented has broader application. Hughes (2006) explained that in 9:6–7, Paul "shows what willing, generous giving is like" (p. 1720). But at a deeper level, it shows what willing, generous *living* is like.

David W. Anderson

Generosity applies to the exercise of all God's gifts, which Paul said in 1 Corinthians 12, are given for the common good; they are to be used, not hoarded. Sharing financially to meet the physical needs of others is important, but generosity is an attitude modeled on Jesus, who generously and graciously gave himself for us. Hence, generosity also applies to our sharing of the gospel, in words and actions, as a conduit of God's love and grace, freely given to us and faithfully passed along to others. Paul wrote in 9:6 that sowing sparingly leads to reaping sparingly. Not sharing from the bounty God has given us, physically and spiritually, cuts us off from God's fullness and blessing, and cuts others off, especially those dealing with disability who also need the good news of the gospel presented verbally, and more importantly, through acceptance and fellowship. Individuals and families facing issues of disability are spiritually hurting. Churches that ignore them in their outreach and service – or blame them for unconfessed sin "causing" or "sustaining" the disability – can create or reinforce feelings of hopelessness and cut them off from God, who is the "source" of blessing.

Generous giving of money, assuming that is what people with disabilities need most, can make the giver feel good but create a spiritual barrier between the giver and the recipient since the person who is disabled is still kept at arm's length. The principle of generosity is not restricted to giving with the hand (funds or hand-me-downs) but includes giving with the heart. Such giving may be in the form of spending time, showing interest, building relationships, and simply sharing life together. These are gifts people who deal with disability need to receive. In building relationships with them, nondisabled persons will also be gifted by God as they serve. Through their openness, they will receive the gift of friendship from individuals and families dealing with disability as lives are shared. Giving of this kind is an expression of love. Simply giving financially does not communicate love, even if the amount is substantial. To restrict "giving" to providing financial assistance or merely spending time when convenient, rather than to relationship-building, creates a separation between nondisabled and disabled persons and families, especially if those individuals and families feel that they are simply a "project." And unloving attitudes of nondisabled persons may lead to thinking they are better than those with a disability or to believe they have done the disabled person a favor. Such thoughts divorce the actions from grace and are displeasing to God.

The principle that giving and reaping are in balance – either both sparingly or both generously (9:6) – connects action with attitude. Whether momentarily or with time and presence, lavish giving is not done for a reward or to put us on display. Joyfulness in giving reflects the condition of the heart. Generosity in giving is never done out of compulsion or to have the spotlight focus on us. MacArthur (2003) wrote, "While it is possible to give without loving, it is not possible to love without giving" (p. 315). God provides for us, not so that we become rich, but so we can be rich in sharing with others. In describing the righteous man, the psalmist wrote, "He has distributed freely; he has given to the poor; his righteousness endures forever; his horn is exalted in honor" (Psalm 112:9). The importance of generous giving or sharing with those in need is also shown in Jesus's affirmation of the second great commandment, "you shall love your neighbor as yourself" (Matthew 22:38, quoting Leviticus 19:18). God himself set the standard for cheerful giving and cheerful living. Paul said God loves a cheerful giver (9:12) because he is himself a cheerful giver: God's gift is inexpressible (9:15); "No language can praise it enough!" (Peterson, 2020, *The Message*). Grace, generosity, and gratitude are not optional elements; they are the essence of Christian living (Wright, 2004). Deuteronomy 15:10–11 supports the principle of generous giving and living, which Paul espoused:

> You shall give to [a poor brother] freely, and your heart shall not be grudging when you give to him, because for this the Lord your God will bless you in all your work and in all that you undertake. For there will never cease to be poor in the land. Therefore I command you, 'You shall open wide your hand to your brother, to the needy and to the poor, [and we can add, to the disabled] in your land.'

As we extend grace to individuals and families dealing with disability (or to anyone, for that matter), we do not "lose" or use up what grace we have; God gives us more grace: we will be *"enriched in every way to be generous in every way"* (9:11). The result, said Paul, will be thanksgiving to God (9:11), glory to God (9:13), and bonding of believers (9:16). Recognizing that God has given and continues to give grace to us as believers should motivate us to be gracious, loving, and generous to others, both able-bodied and disabled. Following the example of Christ, our desire should be to "lavish whatever we can on others for the sake of the gospel" (Millar, 2020, p. 131).

Gospel integrity requires harmony between what we believe and how we live. Moving beyond ourselves and being gracious and giving to others glorifies God. Millar (2020) wrote, "Paul's idea is that Christian believers would choose to put others first, caring for each other when they can – in a kind of grace-driven equilibrium, where everyone is looking out the other people" (p. 130). Few Christians question this, but some are still reluctant to show grace to specific people groups, such as individuals and families who deal with disability. Graciously giving of time and presence can be a simple as pushing a wheelchair, guiding someone who is visually impaired, or making room for an individual who is disabled to sit next to you in the pew. The goal in serving others is not to earn their gratitude but for God to receive glory as a result of our submission and generosity (9:13). Building a relationship with a family that is dealing with disability allows us to know (not assume) their struggles and their needs so we can respond appropriately. But since we are *serving them*, we must avoid the idea that we know what is needed or what help they and the disabled individual genuinely need.

One result of developing a generous relationship with individuals and families who deal with disability is our own spiritual growth. Mike Cope's (2011) daughter, Megan, was born with significant medical issues and lived only to the age of 10. He described his daughter as a quiet and loving witness to the gospel – "an incarnation of God's love" (p. 25). Megan helped him understand God as a "heart specialist." She helped him to know that "what really matters has to do with the heart: keeping promises, seeking justice in a brutal world, leaning to see those in greatest need, and living with courage, joy, and unconditional love" (p. 29). This is a lesson we all need.

LIVING OUTWARDLY AND DESTROYING STRONGHOLDS

For though we walk in the flesh, we are not waging war according to the flesh. For the weapons of our warfare are not of the flesh but have divine power to destroy strongholds.⁵We destroy arguments and every lofty opinion raised against the knowledge of God, and take every thought captive to obey Christ, being ready to punish every disobedience, when your obedience is complete. Look at what is before your eyes. If anyone is confident that he is Christ's, let him remind himself that just as he is Christ's, so also are we. For even if I boast a little too much of our authority, which the Lord gave for building you up and not for destroying you, I will not be ashamed. I do not want to appear to be frightening you with my letters. For they say, "His letters are weighty and strong, but his bodily presence is weak, and his speech of no account." Let such a person understand that what we say by letter when absent, we do when present. Not that we dare to classify or compare ourselves with some of those who are commending themselves. But when they measure themselves by one another and compare themselves with one another, they are without understanding. But we will not boast beyond limits, but will boast only with regard to the area of influence God assigned to us, to reach even to you. For we are not overextending ourselves, as though we did not reach you. For we were the first to come all the way to you with the gospel of Christ. We do not boast beyond limit in the labors of others. But our hope is that as your faith increases, our area of influence among you may be greatly enlarged, so that we may preach the gospel in lands beyond you, without boasting of work already done in another's area of influence. "Let the one who boasts, boast in the Lord." For it is not the one who commends himself who is approved, but the one whom the Lord commends.

2 Corinthians 10:3-18

David W. Anderson

Dahlstrom (2011) asserted that "living outwardly" has always been a critical element of Jesus's vision of following him. As disciples of Jesus, we trust in God's active involvement in our daily lives, in submission to and dependence upon him. From this place of security, we are "invited to live outwardly, finding creative ways to spill hope into the world" (Dahlstrom, p. 15). We *embody* hope and *spill* hope into the lives of others through our words and actions, lovingly serving others.

Individuals and families caught up in the issues accompanying disability often have a diminished sense of hope in their "world," especially if they feel cut off from fellowship with others in society and the church or become entangled in the technicalities of disability and rehabilitation. In Micah 6:8, we are told that God requires us to do justice, love kindness, and walk humbly with God. Dahlstrom (2011) applied this to learning how to live fully through times of pain and comfort, joy and sorrow, peace and turmoil, prosperity and adversity, certainty and doubt. Everyone experiences these highs and lows at times, but families dealing with disability often experience the "lows" more frequently and persistently, depending on the degree of disability and the level of physical, emotional, and spiritual support received from others, especially from the church. Dahlstrom considered justice, mercy, and love the "primary colors" from which hope springs. Christians are the artists who paint the lives of individuals and families dealing with disability with these colors.

In 2 Corinthians 10, Paul again focused on pride and boasting among some in the church at Corinth and on spiritual warfare. Self-pride and boastfulness can disrupt any ministry by highlighting the weakness and vulnerability of some, thereby creating division rather than reconciliation and fellowship. Such attitudes are impediments to ministry to and with individuals and families impacted by disability. Much of what Paul writes in this passage serves as a corrective to those who disregard (or discard) families in which disability plays a large part. Paul's call for breaking down strongholds (10:11) applies to the stronghold of ability which fosters negative attitudes toward weakness and disability. At the same time, Paul's teaching is instructive for the individuals and families directly impacted by disability who, because of the negativity of nondisabled persons in the church, feel entrapped, ignored, or shut out by the church and by society. The principle of taking every thought captive to obey Christ (10:5) applies to both able-bodied nay-sayers and those whose struggles include disability and negativity from the world. The compassion which Jesus modeled toward persons who were disabled is an example for the church today.

Paul's teaching in 10:3–5 placed these issues within the context of spiritual warfare. His comments parallel Ephesians 6:10–20, generally thought written about four years after Corinthians. The Ephesians passage describes the weapons of spiritual warfare. In contrast, the focus of 2 Corinthians 10 is more directly on what the weapons are used for: battling ideas, arguments, philosophies, and world views that are opposed to the true knowledge of God. Barnett (1988) attributed the humanly oriented ideas of the Corinthians to "the entrenched power of unbelief and pride in the human mind" (p. 158). He argued that only the right weapons could overcome this unbelief and pride, the right weapons being the words of the gospel (p. 159).

In the context of disability, four types of strongholds identified by Paul in 10:4–7 need to be destroyed:

1. Negative, prejudicial attitudes toward disability and people who have a disability
2. Arguments against the knowledge of God, such as disability being God's punishment for sin, which makes God unjust. Paul said in Romans 3:22-23, "There is no distinction: for all have sinned and fall short of the glory of God." But if disability is punishment for sin, why are not all people disabled? Is there are certain degree of sinfulness necessary to "cause" a person to be disabled?
3. False thoughts which need to be taken captive to obey Christ include ignoring people with disabilities or attributing responsibility for a disability to unconfessed wrongdoing, thereby placing limits on God's love and ignoring Jesus's command to take the gospel to every people group (Matthew 28:18–20).
4. Not recognizing believers who are disabled to be as much a part of the family of God as those who are nondisabled. Paul wrote, "If anyone is confident that he is Christ's, let him remind himself that just as he is Christ's, so also are we" (10:7). The "we" can include believers who are disabled, placing nondisabled and disabled believers on an even keel.

David W. Anderson

Paul said we must take captive every thought to obey Christ (10:5). While generally familiar with this verse, many Christians are unaware of how our thoughts – in our focus, thoughts regarding disability and people who have a disability – are not captive to Christ but follow worldly ideas and worldly strongholds. Peterson's (2002) paraphrase of this verse shows its application to disability ministry: "We use our powerful God-tools for smashing warped philosophies, tearing down barriers erected against the truth of God, fitting every loose thought and emotion and impulse into the structure of life shaped by Christ" (*The Message*). Though we have divine power – the God-given tools to take captive and demolish these thoughts – we often fail to use them consistently or consciously.

Paul's concern in 10:12 was with comparing ourselves with people who put themselves forward as being "something," saying to do so shows a lack of understanding. Millar (2020) affirmed that comparing ourselves to others is to "throw living by grace through faith out the window and start to run with a gospel of good works" (p. 151). We are not to put ourselves in league with those who boast that they are superior by using words or actions which place us above ("better than") people who are disabled (a backhanded way of putting down those with disability). In comparing ourselves to people we believe are lesser than us, we either do not understand or openly ignore the fact of God's grace. Proper boasting, Paul said, is in the Lord (10:17), not in ourselves, adding, "It is not the one who commends himself who is approved, but the one whom the Lord commends" (10:18). An elitist attitude among nondisabled persons conveys either outright rejection of people with a disability or judge them to be of lesser value and importance. Some may tolerate the presence of a person with a disability, but seldom is a relationship established as equals before the Lord. The question is one of who's approval is correct, the nondisabled person's or God's. "The battle for the mind remains central to the church's task in this and every age" (Wright, 2004, p. 107). In our focus, the battle of the mind is central to welcoming and relating to individuals and families who live with disability, a major obstacle to thinking more highly about ourselves than we ought. Paul wrote a similar instruction to the Christians in Rome, showing the connection of humility to grace and the oneness of the body of Christ:

For by the grace given to me I say to everyone among you not to think of himself more highly than he ought to think, but to think with sober judgment, each according to the measure of faith that God has assigned. For as in one body we have many members, and the members do not all have the same function, so we, though many, are one body in Christ, and individually members one of another. (Romans 12:3–5)

Pridefulness implies an inflated opinion of self-importance, resulting in people with disabilities being overlooked and the view that ministry to and with persons with a disability is unimportant and unnecessary. It also implies catering to the "beautiful, intelligent, and powerful" people who can assist the church should the need occur and attract others of the same ilk to become part of the church. People with disabilities often have a more honest and accurate understanding of themselves – their weakness, their need for others, their need for the Lord – than people who are nondisabled and successful in the world. They may, then, be a good model for nondisabled persons of trust-full Christian living.

Paul's critics dismissed him because of his weak bodily presence, which, in their judgment, was unimpressive and because his speech was "of no account" (10:10). They likely were comparing him to the rhetorical style of Greek scholars, but it is also possible that Paul had some disability; the criticism of his appearance and performance as a preacher resembles comments about people with a disability. MacArthur (2003) pointed out that false teachers typically bring discord or disunity to the church. Churches can be weakened or destroyed by nondisabled people who display a negative attitude toward people-groups they find objectionable. Millar (2020) makes the point clear:

> Every time we look at another person and measure ourselves against them – we are throwing the door wide open to pride … Every time we compare, we throw living by grace through faith out the window and start to run with a gospel of good works. Every time we compare, we swap living to please God with living to please ourselves, under the guise of impressing other people" (p. 151).

Paul displayed pastoral responsibility in correcting the thinking of the Corinthians, destroying strongholds (10:4) that had taken hold in their hearts and thinking. We should do no less today regarding strongholds that oppose people with disabilities and deny the need to include these folks in our ministry.

In Christ, there is no distinction between nondisabled and disabled Christians. We must not neglect graciously serving, welcoming, and having fellowship with individuals and families with disabilities. Nor should we back away if another Christian (or an unbeliever) challenges our actions, attitudes, and ministry toward people with disabilities. Boasting in the Lord is legitimate, for our life as a believer is based on his love and grace. But we cannot pat ourselves on the back for "good deeds" we are doing, and if those good deeds are reaching out and sharing love and life with persons who are disabled, we are doing what is right. Millar (2020) put it well: "When God works, he does so freely and graciously through the gospel by the power of the Spirit in broken people like us, rather than through human giftedness" (p. 145). As Paul warned the Galatians, anyone who thinks he is something, when he is nothing, deceives himself (Galatians 6:3).

WEAKNESS AND THORNS

Who is weak, and I am not weak? Who is made to fall, and I am not indignant? If I must boast, I will boast of the things that show my weakness. ... I must go on boasting. Though there is nothing to be gained by it, I will go on to visions and revelations of the Lord. I know a man in Christ who fourteen years ago was caught up to the third heaven – whether in the body or out of the body I do not know, God knows. And I know that this man was caught up into paradise – whether in the body or out of the body I do not know, God knows – and he heard things that cannot be told, which man may not utter. 5On behalf of this man I will boast, but on my own behalf I will not boast, except of my weaknesses – though if I should wish to boast, I would not be a fool, for I would be speaking the truth; but I refrain from it, so that no one may think more of me than he sees in me or hears from me. So to keep me from becoming conceited because of the surpassing greatness of the revelations, a thorn was given me in the flesh, a messenger of Satan to harass me, to keep me from becoming conceited. Three times I pleaded with the Lord about this, that it should leave me. But he said to me, "My grace is sufficient for you, for my power is made perfect in weakness." Therefore I will boast all the more gladly of my weaknesses, so that the power of Christ may rest upon me. For the sake of Christ, then, I am content with weaknesses, insults, hardships, persecutions, and calamities. For when I am weak, then I am strong. ... For he was crucified in weakness, but lives by the power of God. For we also are weak in him, but in dealing with you we will live with him by the power of God.

2 Corinthians 11:29–30, 12:1–10, 13:4

David W. Anderson

2 Corinthians is a more personal letter as Paul talks about his ministry – his motives, spiritual passion, and love for the church. In 2 Corinthians 11:29–30, Paul expressed his deep love and concern for the believers in Corinth, evidenced by his ongoing relationship with them. The NASB translation of these verses brings out more clearly the depth of Paul's connection to the people: "Who is weak without my being weak? Who is led into sin without my intense concern?" This same tenderhearted concern for believers was characteristic of Paul's relationship with others he had ministered to (e.g., Galatians 4:19, 1 Thessalonians 2:7–9).

That Paul boasted in things that manifest his weakness (11:30) is neither prideful nor designed to garner sympathy. Paul boasted in his weakness so that Christ would receive the praise for what had been accomplished through his ministry. This reveals Paul's countercultural thinking. Many people like to be noticed and receive congratulatory pats on the back. But, like Paul, any achievement we have flows from and through Christ. People with a disability may have an advantage in this regard; they know their weaknesses and limitation, whereas nondisabled people try to hide or deny theirs. Some nondisabled people "serve," hoping to be noticed and verbally rewarded. Those with a disability may be more godly and humble in their service, doing it not to be seen but to serve as Jesus served.

"The persistent motif of authentic ministry is *power in weakness*" (Hughes, 2006, p. 213) and runs throughout Paul's epistles to the Corinthian church (1 Corinthians 1:27–29, 2:3–5, 9:22–23, 12:22–26; 2 Corinthians 4:7–12). Paul is an example of how God does not work in ways the world thinks best, boasting in his weakness, through which the power of Christ is released. Weakness (or disability) removes "us" from the equation as we acknowledge our dependence on God as our source of strength, joy, and purpose. What the world considers weak and insignificant is precisely what God wants to use because the glory is his, not ours.

This paradox of strength through weakness points to the greatness of God, who resists the proud and gives grace to the humble (James 4:6). From a human perspective, those who are weak are the least likely candidates for kingdom work. Human reasoning suggests that "weaker" church members, including those with a disability, are of lesser importance or value and perhaps should be kept hidden from view. A worldly focus is on people who demonstrate giftedness through performance: powerful preaching, insightful teaching, or musical talent. But when seen with spiritual eyes, valuing what God values, weaker members of the body of Christ become a platform by which God can advance his kingdom and display his glory; they are indispensable to Christ's mission through the church (1 Corinthians 12:23).

The Corinthians were preoccupied with external appearances and the spectacular; they liked a "good show." False teachers in Corinth were eloquent and impressive speakers, able to lure others into following unbiblical ideas which emphasized ritual, special knowledge, and dramatic spiritual experiences. They questioned Paul's credentials, challenging his integrity and authority as an apostle, labeling him insincere, spiritually weak, careless in handling money, and a poor public speaker. Paul confronted the Corinthians about their fascination with false teachers and defended his apostolic authority, though he knew there is no profit in bragging. He strongly affirmed the legitimacy of his apostleship but felt having to defend himself, and his love was "foolishness" (11:1). What mattered most to Paul was not his achievement but what God was doing through him and the gospel. Reluctant to engage in a contest of personalities, he boasted in his weakness rather than his accomplishments. Thorn, weakness, grace, and power are key words in his response.

Paul said he has a "thorn in the flesh," a messenger of Satan sent to continually torment him, perhaps something that came frequently and unexpectedly to quash any pretension of working in his own strength. Satan intended to prevent the spread of the gospel by discouraging Paul and causing people to reject him and his message. Because Paul regarded self-boasting as foolishness, he uses third-person language to describe "a man," a follower of Christ who, 14 years earlier, was transported to the heights of heaven. Whether a physical or spiritual rapture, he is not sure, but the man was "hijacked into Paradise" (Peterson, 2002, *The Message*), where he heard things that cannot be expressed in human words.

Paul's "thorn" has been variously explained. Some connect it to emotional or physical concerns over the state of the church in Corinth, but this, in itself, was probably not Paul's thorn. Perhaps his thorn may have been a physical ailment, something that would be limiting, maybe even painful. The Greek word "thorn" (*skolops*) can be translated as "stake" or "splinter," suggesting Paul may have suffered from severe headaches as if a sharp and pointed bar was thrust into his forehead. Some suggest he dealt with recurring illnesses like malaria or epilepsy or had a speech disorder which led his critics to say "his speech was of no account" (2 Corinthians 10:10), or physical weakness or disability resulting from his imprisonment and beatings (2 Corinthians 6:6, 11:23). Still others propose the thorn consisted of spiritual struggles involving temptations and persecution, perhaps drawing from Numbers 33:55 where "thorn" described enemies who constantly harassed Israel and became barbs in their eyes and thorns in their sides. The possibility of a visual disability is suggested in Galatians 4:13–15 where Paul spoke of the Galatians' willingness to give their eyes to him, and Galatians 6:11 where he referred to writing in "large letters." Whatever the thorn was, Paul found it bothersome, debilitating and perhaps humiliating.

His critics in Corinth likely viewed his disability or weakness with disdain (just as some people today see disability). But Paul came to understand it as evidence of God's presence in his ministry. Not explicitly identifying his "thorn" suggests the Corinthians may have known what he was referring to (MacArthur, 2003). Our not knowing precisely what it was allows every Christian to relate to Paul's teaching and to acknowledge that God's strength is manifested through our weakness, as well.

Paul's "thorn" appears to have been a physical condition evident to all, leading to criticism from his detractors. His repeated prayer that God would remove the thorn suggests a chronic condition, something experienced at least intermittently over a lengthy period with observable and perhaps humiliating symptoms. Initially concerned about his disability, Paul's prayers likely included asking God why he had this thorn or disability. Saying he prayed "three times" for the thorn to be removed indicates the depth of Paul's concern. He may have intentionally been drawing a parallel to Jesus, who prayed three times in the Garden of Gethsemane for God to take away the cup of suffering (Matthew 26:39, 42, 44). While Paul's suffering did not compare to that of Jesus, he was in this way showing his identification with Jesus.

God's answer to Paul's prayer was "no," but God gave a reason for the thorn: "My grace is sufficient for you, for my power is made perfect in [your] weakness" (12:9a). God permitted Satan to afflict Paul with this "thorn." Though Satan's purpose was to prevent the spread of the gospel, God intended the thorn to be a constant reminder to Paul of his weakness or disability to prevent him from becoming prideful. Satan meant the "thorn" as evil, but God made it serve a good purpose: Paul's reliance on God's power.

Once Paul understood God's intent, he saw his "thorn" to be a gift from God to prevent him from working from or trusting in his own strength. Thus, he rejoiced in his weakness so that the power of Christ would rest on him (12:9). His boast was a confession of faith and trust in God and God's will. Understanding that God's grace was involved, his attitude changed to acceptance and thanksgiving.

Paul's experience helps us understand that disability does not prevent happiness; true happiness is knowing God. Paul modeled how any Christian who is or becomes disabled can live a life of righteousness and service. Despite the non-removal of his thorn, Paul's joy stemmed from the security of his relationship with God. God told Paul his grace was all he needed, a promise that in itself is a gift of grace. Knowing God's faithfulness and truthfulness allowed Paul to rest securely in God's presence and grace as he moved forward in his ministry, even with his thorn. God's answer helped Paul realize that serving God does not mean "easy living" and enabled him to continue his mission with more determination, knowing the certainty of God's grace. What he first thought was Satan's harassment, he now understood to be a gift from God preventing him from becoming conceited. God's assuring explanation enabled him to focus, not on his thorn but on God and the promise of grace.

Deuel and John (2019) suggested three reasons for Paul's thorn: to remove prideful thoughts because of the great revelations he had received, to put him in a position of need so he could receive God's help, and to help him recognize that Christ's power was working in him. Working in our strength is not God's desire. Proverbs 3:5–7 tells us to trust in the Lord, not in our own understanding; to acknowledge him in all things and not be wise in our own eyes; to fear the Lord and turn from evil. Our strength is not essential. What is necessary is surrendering to God and trusting in his ability to act in and through us, regardless of our ability or lack thereof.

Through our weakness and limitation, we most clearly experience God's strength. God's power is made perfect (complete) in our weakness;

any "self-power" comes to an end so that God receives honor by acting through us. Relying on self-effort, blinded by our strength, may hinder God's activity. The Greek word translated "weakness" (12:9–10) is *astheneia*, which refers to physical disease or infirmity. This term is used of the man by the pool of Bethesda who had been disabled for 38 years. Yong (2011) suggested the word closely parallels the modern term "disability."

When God looks at a person who is disabled, he does not see a person of limited value but someone through whom he can display his greatness. We are what we are by God's grace, even if that grace entails being disabled. Paul explained in 1 Corinthians 1:27–30 that God uses what the world considers weak, foolish, or despised so that people cannot boast in his presence. Upon encountering the man born blind (John 9), Jesus said the man's blindness provided an opportunity for the works of God to be displayed. The work of God was the man's coming to faith; his cure from blindness was a bonus: his salvation was not dependent on the cure.

God often used "weaker" individuals to play a critical role in accomplishing his will for Israel and the church: Joseph, a presumptuous youth raised by God to be prime minister of Egypt (Genesis 37, 39–50); Moses, whose speech impediment presented no obstacle to God's rescuing his people from Egyptian bondage (Exodus 4:8); David, the youngest son of Jesse, who Samuel anointed to be king of Israel (1 Samuel 17:40–50); Mary, a young unwed maiden who gave birth to the Savior (Luke, 1:26–38); a little child, used by Jesus to teach a lesson on humility (Matthew 18:1–6); and Jesus's disciples, ordinary men who "turned the world upside down" (Acts 17:6). Beates (2012) asserted, "God's story in Scripture uses these characters to highlight their weakness, their inability, their brokenness. And in so doing, God's glory and God's grace are magnified all the more!" (p. 25).

Carlson (1994) wrote, "Paul experienced God's sufficiency … by being able to handle the weakness or deficiency in an appropriate way and by seeing more clearly that it was God who worked through him and in him" (p.36). Weakness is part of God's plan for his children because it leads us to depend on God. "We cannot appreciate God's strength and his glorious purposes unless we first experience our own weakness" (Deuel & John, 2019, p. 14).

Christians sometimes restrict "grace" to apply only to salvation and justification. Paul helps us see grace in broader terms in 2 Corinthians 12. God's answer to Paul's repeated prayer essentially was "No." God explained, "My grace is sufficient for you, for my powers is made perfect in weakness" (12:9). "Sufficient" (Greek = arkei) can be simply translated as "enough," which seems a stronger term, as we sometimes use it in a forceful way reflecting exasperation or annoyance ("enough!"). Peterson's (2002) paraphrase reads, "My grace is enough; it's all you need. My strength comes into its own in your weakness" (*The Message*).

Grace is all we need for salvation, but it is also God's provision for living the Christian life, which we cannot do in our own strength; it requires the enabling power of God. Being a good soldier of Christ necessitates continual strengthening by the grace that is in Christ Jesus (2 Timothy 2:1). In the same way that the gospel message is not to be kept to ourselves but taken to the whole world, God's grace is not something we keep to ourselves or rest in (in the sense of idleness) but is to flow through us to others. Paul's statement in 1 Corinthians 15:30, "I am what I am," was not simply an acknowledgment that it was God's grace that made him a Christian. His thought is comprehensive, applying to what he is each day, what he does each day, and how he lives each day. Paul said grace even informs how we evaluate ourselves and others (Romans 12:3). When we encounter someone who is disabled, especially severely disabled, our eyes, attitude, and acceptance must exhibit grace, just as Jesus did when coming across persons who were disabled. It pleases God when we show grace and compassion to others, nondisabled or disabled, modeling Jesus through our actions. To not include disabled individuals in our worship and fellowship dishonors them, but it also dishonors God, whose love is not limited to certain types of people. The same "nourishing and cherishing" Paul spoke of in Ephesians 5:29–30 is to be shared with every member of Christ's body, and perhaps especially with those dealing with disability who often feel they are on the outskirts of the church community.

When encountering someone with a severe physical or intellectual disability, some people voice questions that distance them from that person: Why is she like that? What's wrong with him? Seldom do they ask, "What's *right* with that person?" Kovac (2013) wrote, "My parents taught me that I may have a disability, but I'm not 'disabled.' Not one of us is perfect. And that's OK. What's *not* OK is letting our flaws define us" (p. 19). A wrong attitude toward disability on the part of individual Christians, or the church as a whole, prevents people from becoming all God wants them to be. How might Paul's ministry have been different if he did not learn to see his disability as a gracious gift from God? Might he have given up his ministry?

In Luke 18:15–17, we read that Jesus's disciples tried to prevent parents from bringing infants and young children to Jesus so he might bless them. Jesus reprimanded the disciples saying, "let the children come to me, do not hinder them, for to such belongs the kingdom of God; whoever does not receive the kingdom of God like a child shall not enter it." I believe Jesus is equally unhappy when churches or individual Christians turn away people with disabilities. Kinard (2019) asks rhetorically, "Did [the disciples] think Jesus has more important things to do? Did the disciples think they were protecting Jesus from distractions?" (54). Similarly, do we need to protect God, the church leaders, and the congregation from the distraction of people who are disabled? Are there other groups of people we need to shield God from? Did Jesus make any exceptions regarding whom we share the gospel with? In Jesus's parable of the final judgment (Matthew 25:31–48), he lists hungry, thirsty, strangers, the naked, and imprisoned, saying "as you did it to one of the least of these my brothers, you did it to me." Nondisabled people often see people with disabilities as "strangers" and the isolation they feel because of negative attitudes of able-bodied "imprisoning." That Jesus did not specifically include the disabled in this list does not permit us to ignore them.

To say God's power is made perfect in weakness seems nonsense to the world, but God's power and our weakness tie to God's grace. God gave Paul grace in his "handicap," saying that God's strength is more fully displayed through Paul's weakness. In 12:9, the Greek literally reads, "Sufficient for you is my grace, for the power [strength] in weakness is perfected." "Perfected" can mean something is *made perfect* or something *is finished or completed*. Understood the first way, it applies to God's power being made perfect; God's power is demonstrated as he works through Paul's inabilities. Understood the second way, it applies to Paul's power being brought to an end by his weakness: Paul cannot boast of his deeds because *his* power is "ended" or "finished." Either understanding leads to the same result: Paul is weak or powerless, but Christ, by his strength, makes Paul strong. God's power is best displayed against the background of human weaknesses.

Many Christians incorrectly believe Christ will deliver them from all trouble and hardship. He certainly could do this, but he has never promised this. Paul said God's power is often given *in the midst of* our weakness or handicap. Some Christians spend time, effort, and money seeking a physical cure and become discouraged or lose faith if God chooses not to cure them. But as Scazzero (2017) said, "The strength [Paul] received from Christ was not the strength to change, deny, or defy his circumstances; it was the strength to be content in the midst of them, to surrender to God's loving will for him" (p. 36).

Hughes (2006) suggested that this power paradox – "my weakness plus his strength equals his power" (p. 215) – should be a pattern for Christian living. Human power or strength is not the same as God's power or strength. God is omnipotent; our power is fragile and fleeting. Our weakness provides the opportunity for God to demonstrate his power. Wright (2004) said our power must be "knocked out of the way" so that God's power can "shine through as God desires and intends" (p. 133).

Paul wrote that God is a God who comforts so that those he comforts can comfort others (2 Corinthians 1:4). In 12:7–10, Paul helps us understand that "comfort" does not mean removing a disability, but spiritual strengthening *in* and *through* disability. Having a physical or intellectual disability does not imply a person is spiritually weak. Their witness may actually be more robust than that of nondisabled persons who believe themselves to be strong. Serving from the heart, in whatever capacity and with whatever spiritual gift we have, is strength. Weakness turns our eyes from self to grace.

God will have no strength used in his battles except the strength which he gives. The weaker the instrument God uses the more God's power and grace are demonstrated for all to see. Recognizing that God works through seemingly weak persons should help us see people with disabilities more positively. Paul's teaching in 2 Corinthians 12 links to what he wrote in 1 Corinthians 1:26–31 about God working in and through weakness rather than human strength. Paul helps us understand that disability is not necessarily something to be gotten rid of; it can be a vessel by which God can bring blessing to people and glory to himself as a testimony to his grace and provision. Reimer (2019) said the real question to be asked is, "How can we help our friends with special needs to be involved in the Great Commission?" (p. 132).

Paul's perspective on the thorn and his weakness was changed by God's grace. What he naturally found distressing, limiting, and perhaps painful he could welcome because, in the end, it brings greater glory to God. Rather than removing the problem, God gave Paul grace *in* the problem, transforming how he saw his weakness or disability and enabling him to "boast" in his weakness. As Paul said in Romans 8:28, "We know that for those who love God all things work together for good, for those who are called according to his purpose." "All things" includes disability.

We must not assume a person being cured or not cured of a disability is a reflection of their faith; being cured depends on God's sovereign will. Paul learned that God's grace is sufficient, that God's power increases as Paul's weakness grows. Hence, there is no reason for Paul to ask for the removal of the thorn. The gift of Paul's disability was achieving its intended goal.

Paul's response to God's revelation was, "I will boast all the more gladly about my weaknesses, so that Christ's power may rest on me … for Christ's sake, I delight in weaknesses, in insults, in hardships, in persecutions, in difficulties. For when I am weak, then I am strong" (12:9–10). Paul understood from this revelation that it was a privilege to be afflicted, handicapped, or disabled because then there is more abundant blessing from God: Christ's power *rests* (dwells, tabernacles) on him.

The same power Christ demonstrated during his ministry and the same power from God that raised Christ from the grave abides with Paul in his weakness and with us in our weakness. Thus, Paul could rejoice in his infirmity, and so can we. The point of our weakness is the gracious indwelling of Christ's power, enabling us to say, "I can do everything through him who gives me strength" (Philippians 4:13). Paul's weakness became a showplace for God's grace and power to be displayed.

In our weakness, we most clearly experience God's strength because our weakness becomes an opportunity for God to display his power. Human nature leads us to attempt to work on our own, and we sometimes succeed, but the result is pride and self-satisfaction. When we are weak, we depend on God to fill us with his power, making us stronger than we could ever be on our own. Our dependence on God in our weakness l contributes to growth in Christian character and deeper worship as we witness how he works through our weakness.

The greatest picture of power in weakness is Christ's incarnation and crucifixion. Jesus was crucified in weakness but lives by God's power (Philippians 2:7–8). Likewise, we are weak in him, yet we live for him and serve others (2 Corinthians 13:4).

Paul's assurance of God's presence in his weakness and inability helps us understand the indispensable role of those who appear less able but are nonetheless an essential part of the body of Christ. People with disabilities are not objects of shame and guilt, nor people to be gotten rid of, hidden away, or kept at a distance. Weakness is indispensable to the life of the church. Weakness and disability lead us to trust and depend on God. His weakness and inability handicapped Paul, but Christ's power dwells and flourishes in him. Consequently, when he is weak, he is strong because of Christ's power working in and through him.

Dying to the attempt to accomplish God's purposes through our power is part of the gospel of grace. God wants our weakness, not any strength we have. Our "power" becomes a rival to God, who will not share his glory with anyone or anything. "The church is constituted first and foremost of the weak, not the strong: people with disabilities are thus at the center rather than at the margins of what it means to be the people of God" (Yong, 2011, p. 95).

KOINONIA AND HOSPITALITY

But in the following instructions I do not commend you, because when you come together it is not for the better but for the worse. For in the first place, when you come together as a church, I hear that there are divisions among you. And I believe it in part, for there must be factions among you in order that those who are genuine among you may be recognized. When you come together, it is not the Lord's supper that you eat. For in eating, each one goes ahead with his own meal. One goes hungry, another gets drunk. What! Do you not have houses to eat and drink in? Or do you despise the church of God and humiliate those who have nothing? What shall I say to you? Shall I commend you in this? No, I will not. For I received from the Lord what I also delivered to you, that the Lord Jesus on the night when he was betrayed took bread, and when he had given thanks, he broke it, and said, "This is my body, which is for you. Do this in remembrance of me." In the same way also he took the cup, after supper, saying, "This cup is the new covenant in my blood. Do this, as often as you drink it, in remembrance of me." For as often as you eat this bread and drink the cup, you proclaim the Lord's death until he comes. Whoever, therefore, eats the bread or drinks the cup of the Lord in an unworthy manner will be guilty concerning the body and blood of the Lord. Let a person examine himself, then, and so eat of the bread and drink of the cup. For anyone who eats and drinks without discerning the body eats and drinks judgment on himself. That is why many of you are weak and ill, and some have died. But if we judged ourselves truly, we would not be judged. But when we are judged by the Lord, we are disciplined so that we may not be condemned along with the world. So then, my brothers, when you come together to eat, wait for one another – if anyone is hungry, let him eat at home – so that when you come together it will not be for judgment.

1 Corinthians 11:17-34a

This passage is very familiar to Christians, as portions of it are often read when gathering around the Lord's Table to celebrate communion. I have chosen to deal with these words from Paul last because it again focuses our attention on unity and oneness in the body of Christ. Paul addressed divisiveness in the church in 1 Corinthians 1:10 and addressed it often in both Corinthian epistles. His words were designed to correct the Corinthians' theology and practice because they had allowed divisions to disrupt relationships among the believers. The focus of Paul's attention was their church gatherings for a "love feast," during which time they would celebrate Communion, but we can apply his concern to any fellowship gathering of believers. Paul's specific concern was a division between rich and poor members of the fellowship. Though intended to be a gathering of the family of God in Corinth, the fact that the wealthy separated themselves for the meal belied the unity that should characterize people of faith. Based on externals, such a separation displayed a rift, or schism, in the church – not over theology but over behavior which reflected misdirection in the practical outworking of theology. The effect was to disrupt or destroy unity in the body of Christ. The wealthy came to the meal with ample food, but instead of the meal being shared among everyone, the rich separated themselves from the poorer members, calling attention to the division based on wealth and poverty, in effect humiliating those who had little. Rather than displaying grace, the poor were dis-graced by the wealthy, whose behavior did not correspond to the theology of oneness in Christ.

Paul condemned this behavior because it did more harm than good (11:17). Prejudice on the part of the wealthy disrupted what was intended to be a fellowship of believers. The self-willed division indicated class distinctions were being made by the more affluent members, whose actions revealed a favorable judgment of themselves but a negative assessment of the poor. Wilson (1972) concluded, "The loveless abuse of the Love-feast in Corinth was a blatant denial of the fellowship which this common meal was intended to express" (p. 166). Though meant to be a love feast, it became a loveless feast, in which the "haves" (the wealthy) were honored, but the "have-nots" (the poor) were dishonored. In so doing, they also dishonored Christ, who makes no distinction among the parts of his body, the church, just as the parts of our physical body do not withdraw from their union with other body parts.

David W. Anderson

To Paul, this division stemmed from false teaching, which separated people based on social status. Parallel behavior is at play when nondisabled members of the church separate themselves from or act un-gracefully toward, their brothers and sisters in Christ who deal with issues of disability in their family. This response often stems from social or theological stigma associated with disability, which reflects inaccurate information and theology of disability. Just as with Paul's criticism of separation by class standards, discrimination against and separation from people who deal with disability disrupts unity, revealing pride and its twin brother, prejudice.

When Christ instituted the Lord's Supper, his instruction was to "do this in remembrance of me." He was not simply saying we remember him when partaking of the elements representing his body and blood, shed for all who believe. The bread and the juice do, of course, remind us of his sacrificial death. But because Jesus's sacrifice was for *all* believers, celebrating communion is, in a sense, a "re–membering" of Jesus, declaring our union with him in his death and resurrection, and the unity of all God's people, from any racial, ethnic, socioeconomic, or dis/ability group. It entails recalling what Jesus has done and highlights the unity of all who believe; a re–membering with Christ and with other believers because, in Christ, we are one body, united with Christ and with each other. Jesus said a house divided against itself will not be able to stand (Mark 3:25). Jesus was not speaking specifically about the church, but the principle applies: the body of Christ is one. The divisions in the church at Corinth weakened the whole body. As with making a distinction between wealthy and needy church members, a division between able-bodied and disabled also undermines the church and its testimony. In the church at Corinth, this division negated any sense of community or family. It gave visual evidence of disunity and insensitivity to the physical needs of the poor (Prior, 1985). What was intended as a visual demonstration of a covenant community belonging to the Lord was undermined by the behavior of the more wealthy believers, or in our focus, the able-bodied believers,

Webb-Mitchell (2010) showed how this oneness within the body of Christ applies to the relationship between disabled and nondisabled persons, based on a new body politic in which able-bodied ("the valuable") are not separated from the disabled ("the less valuable"). Both groups are equal in the body of Christ as a result of the Holy Spirit's work. Regardless of how the world defines people, able-bodied or disabled, "our place is equal in worth, value, respect, and honor, to each and every other part of the body of Christ" (Webb-Mitchell, p. 65). As with the parts of the human body, all believers are equally part of the body of Christ connected with and necessary to the whole body, regardless of ability or disability, and each has a vital role in the body (as in 1 Corinthians 12).

McCloughry and Morris (2002) wrote that Christ calls Christians into a community established on *God's*, not human criteria. Those whom God calls to be united are to destroy anything that separates people, but this does not mean everyone is to conform to some standard of "sameness." Individuality is not lost, but our lives are re-purposed to bring glory to God. Including people with disabilities as equal parts of the church shows the global nature of Christ's kingdom and the broadness of God's love – *all* in Christ are part of his body.

In 1 Corinthians 1:9, Paul wrote, "God is faithful, by whom you were called into the fellowship of his Son, Jesus Christ our Lord." The Greek word translated "fellowship" is koinonia. Koinonia is demonstrated by showing love and concern for others, using our spiritual gifts, and giving physical assistance, such as sharing food, spending time, and financial aid as the need arises. Koinonia deepens as Jesus's command to love one another as he has loved us (John 13:34) becomes standard practice. Concerning ministry to, with, and among individuals and families dealing with disabilities, love begins by giving acceptance and encouragement, not out of compulsion or to bring attention to ourselves, but in remembrance of Jesus: willingly, joyfully, enthusiastically, and humbly, neither forcing ourselves on others nor deciding what they need based on our experience. We do it out of love for the Lord and others, honoring those we serve and the One we serve.

Koinonia is more than just a friend or a loosely understood gathering of believers. Koinonia describes an intimate unity, a spiritual oneness, among believers and between believers and the Lord (Brodie, 2021). Paul said this was missing because of the division among believers, a charge first mentioned in 1 Corinthians 1 and more directly addressed here in 1 Corinthians 11. The absence of koinonia was evidenced by the self-focus of the wealthy, which led to the lack of mutual sharing and a sense of belonging to one another.

A significant ingredient of koinonia and mutual love among believers is embodying hospitality in our interactions with believers and unbelievers alike. The mutual love of believers for one another not only strengthens the church and brings glory to God, but can attract unbelievers to Christ. Hospitality, which is "at the heart of Christian life, drawing from God's grace and reflecting God's graciousness. In hospitality, we respond to the welcome that God has offered and replicate that welcome in the world" (Pohl, 2012, p. 159). Hospitality requires demonstrating God-like compassion and has particular significance, theologically and practically, for ministry to others, especially those dealing with disability. Hospitality gives witness to the authenticity of the gospel. The Greek word translated as "hospitality" or "hospitable" (*philoxenia*) technically means fondness of strangers or guests, and people with a disability. Paul instructed Christians to "practice hospitality" (Romans 12:13) and listed being hospitable among the qualifications for church leaders (1 Timothy 3:2, 5:10; Titus 1:8), which makes hospitality essential even among the laity, from whence leaders are selected. Peter urged hospitality within the context of loving and serving others which brings glory and praise to God (1 Peter 4:8–11).

Christian hospitality images God's acts of hospitality and requires "the creation of a free and friendly space where we can reach out to strangers and invite them to become our friends" (Nouwen, 1975, p. 79). But, Reinders (2008) cautioned, "Space is a *necessary* but not a *sufficient* condition for inclusion" (p. 161). Hospitality is an intentional practice reflecting openness and welcome rather than specific tasks to be performed, and is offered freely and openly.

Hospitality demands that each person, able-bodied and disabled, be seen as an individual created in God's image. This means acknowledging, respecting, and accommodating an individual's impairment and the functional limitation that results. Paul identified the segregation of wealthy and poor as an affront to God and God's family. The same is true if Christians separate those with a disability from the main body of the church. Having a disability does not negate the individual's place at the fellowship table; nondisabled believers must be ready to share that space. A cognitive, affective, or physical/sensory impairment presents some limitation, but the impairment is only one aspect, not the person's totality, and the disability does not affect the person's soul. Pohl's (1995) comment about biblical hospitality brings out its relationship to reconciliation and interdependence:

> Hospitality practices that offer a transforming social network to detached strangers require a heterogeneous community with multiple intersecting relationships and fluid roles ... Without reciprocal relations and commitments, without hosts and guests aware of their need and dependence on one another, relations are flattened and commitments are too thin to give people a place in the world (pp. 134–135).

Reciprocal relationship and community are not what Paul saw happening in the church in Corinth, and that lack is often mirrored in churches today.

Biblical accounts of hospitality focus on entertaining strangers or aliens, people who were vulnerable because of being "outsiders," and potential victims of overt abuse, as in the case of the man who fell among thieves in Jesus's parable of the good Samaritan (Luke 10:25–37), or covert abuse, as in the intentional disregard of that unfortunate man by the priest and Levite who passed by him. Individuals and families affected by disability are also "unseen" or considered outsiders by some believers, leaving them vulnerable to isolation or discrimination. Attitudinal and theological barriers built from fear or ignorance often result in disabled persons not being acknowledged as true peers by those who are nondisabled.

Koinonia and the hospitality it enkindles builds on godly love and mutual respect and promotes deep friendship and solidarity by enabling nondisabled and disabled persons to see and treat each other as equals despite differences in their ability. The biblical principle of loving others as we love ourselves (Matthew 22:39) demands an appreciation of this equality. "The key to unlocking the door of hospitality is maintaining an open and ready heart" (Reynolds, 2006, p. 201). Hospitality is a means of grace for both the giver and receiver of hospitality. Through it, we mediate the love of Christ and "make a powerful statement to the world about who is interesting, valuable, and important to us" (Pohl, 2003, p. 11).

Just as the church is to be "in" koinonia, so the church is to be characterized by hospitality (Romans 12:12; Hebrews 13:2; 1 Peter 4:9). This begins with recognition of our commonalities, not our differences or disability.

CONCLUDING THOUGHTS

Smart (2001) explained that to say something is "normal" is to apply a definition of exclusion: "if deviance, illness, or disability are not present, the person is judged to be normal" (p. 3). "Normal," having no clear and objective definition, falls in the category of "I know it when I see it," or "normal is in the eye of the beholder." Hence, diverse cultures and even different people within the same culture will understand normality and disability differently and falsely believe disability only happens to other people. Thus, "the determination of normalcy and abnormalcy is not an evaluation, because these concepts have no inherent value, but is rather a simple determination based on how typical an event, a characteristic, or a behavior is" (Smart, p. 4). That determination is made from the viewpoint of persons who do not have a visible or culturally defined "abnormality," making it very subjective and evoking a negative assessment of people who are disabled.

But living in a fallen world makes disability, actual or potential, a "normal" part of life. After God created the world, he described it as very good (Genesis 1:31), meaning it was pleasant and agreeable to the senses, and more importantly, to God's intent (Genesis 1:31}. But when Adam and Eve pursued their interests, the world became abnormal, or perhaps more accurately, anti-normal. Brokenness, spiritual and physical (including disability), became the "norm" as "creation was subjected to futility" (Romans 8:20). No one is guaranteed an un-disabled life. We all grow older, we all are subject to illnesses, accidents, and violence which increase the possibility of becoming disabled, and we all die.

The problem highlighted by exploring Paul's teaching from the perspective of disability is that the church has primarily ignored individuals and families who deal with disability, in some cases locating the cause of disability in personal sin and God's judgment, or accusing the disabled person of having insufficient faith to be healed, thereby revealing the normate bias and insensitivity to disability. These attitudes do not display love and compassion toward, but rejection of the person, resulting in the disabled individual rejecting God and the gospel. Some Christians may fail to respond because the brokenness of disability calls attention to the fact that the world is not as it should be and highlights our finiteness, a reality many would rather not face on a personal level (Beates, 2012).

Several themes in Paul's epistles to the Corinthian church have been explored with disability in mind. But Beates' (2012) comment is accurate:

> The absence of people with disabilities in the church indicates that the church has not yet grasped deeply enough the essence of the gospel; and conversely, God's people have drunk too deeply from the well of cultural ideology with regard to wholeness and brokenness. (p. 79)

Paul's rebuke of the church in Corinth was appropriate and applies to today's churches as well. By not reaching out to individuals and families affected by disability, the church fails to obey Jesus's command to take the gospel to all people groups. And by "drinking from the well of cultural ideology," the church neglects its responsibility to care for people who are "broken" due to physical or intellectual impairment and spiritually "broken" because of the perception that God is against them. Overt or covert rejection by the church leaves individuals and families dealing with disability emotionally and spiritually isolated.

Hale (2012) correctly said, "the experience of disability can and should affect our understanding of what it means to be the church" (p. 100). In Luke 4:18–19, Jesus announced his mission was to proclaim good news to the poor, liberty to the captives, recovery of sight to the blind, and liberty to the oppressed. This same ministry is given to every believer, not just missionaries and evangelists. The words "captives" and "oppressed" apply to individuals and families who live with disability and are confronted by cultural attitudes that push them to the margins of society or the church. The church's response, flowing from the Luke 4 mission statement, includes several elements: love, healing, and wholeness; reconciliation; hospitality; building up (edifying) others; and grace.

Love leading to healing and wholeness is to be actively and visibly displayed. In 2 Corinthians 5:14, Paul declared that the love of God controls us – more emphatically, compels us – giving motivation and direction to our actions. Millar (2020) explained that "loving as Christ did is at the core of authentic Christian ministry … [As] our grasp of the gospel increases, then so will our love for other people" (pp. 88–89). "Other people" includes those whose lives are impacted by disability, and provide the opportunity for Christians to demonstrate their love for God by loving them faithfully (cf. Deuel, 2013).

Healing and wholeness emanate from the relationships we seek to develop with people who are disabled and their families as we become vessels through which the love of Christ flows to others. Healing begins by consciously removing barriers that separate able-bodied from disabled people and disabled people from God. Through our ministry to and with persons who deal with disability, characterized and fueled by love, we become agents of God to promote relational and spiritual healing, a sense of wholeness despite being disabled. Paul wrote in 1 Corinthians 13 that love is patient and kind, not arrogant or rude. Healing ensues from engaging in a loving relationship with persons and families dealing with disability. Through our love, we help them understand that the steadfast love of the Lord extends to the heavens, his faithfulness to the clouds; and that because of God's steadfast love, we – able-bodied and disabled – find refuge in the shadow of God's wings (Psalm 36:5 and 7).

Reconciliation with others builds from the love God has shed into our lives, flowing to others through our words and actions. Christians are new creations: enmity with God and others is gone, and a new relationship with God through Christ has begun. This new relationship with God enables having a new relationship with others, including those with disabilities. Being reconciled with God and others is at the core of community, but community does not mean uniformity (Anderson, 2013). Each person is an individual, made in the image of God and uniquely designed, gifted, and purposed by God. Community occurs when we recognize that every person, able-bodied and disabled, is unique and has a gift to offer others. Vanier (1992), who worked with adults with significant disabilities, advocated learning to love difference, to see it as a treasure, not a threat. Without reconciled attitudes, persons with a disability are stripped of their humanity and labeled unworthy, useless, or less than human. But those who "disable" by labeling and segregating people with handicapping conditions also act inhumanely. Their reconciliation begins with being liberated from the assumption that they are "healthy" and fear of becoming disabled. Living in community with persons who are disabled allows us to appreciate the gifts these individuals have and are. This reconciliation is needed both in the church leadership and in the laity, but leaders have a greater responsibility in that their attitude and actions can model for the laity how to interact with persons and families dealing with disability properly.

Hospitality is a rich biblical concept that is of particular significance in ministering to and with persons who deal with issues of disability and is an essential witness to the authenticity of the gospel (Anderson, 2013). In 1993, Roger Badham wrote, "A church that practices any form of exclusivity is predetermining who shall sit at Christ's table ... To fail to open the doors of our churches and our hearts is ultimately a spiritually self-limiting decision" (pp. 238–239). Many churches have a restricted focus that flies in the face of Jesus's teaching in Luke 14:1–24. When in the home of a prominent Pharisee, Jesus observed people coming to the banquet table, each seeking a position of honor. He told the guests that giving a party for relatives and friends may bring earthly reward, as they reciprocate by inviting you to their home. Better, said Jesus, to invite people who are not in a position to return the favor, as this will lead to eternal reward. To help the guests and the host understand his meaning, Jesus told the parable of the "great banquet" to which guests who had accepted the invitation refused to come. As a result, their place at the table was given to the poor and disabled; people thought unworthy and undeserving. The parable reveals an element of surprise to the Kingdom of God: many who think they will be included will be left out, and those who are included are people some would least expect.

The church needs to be a welcoming community into which persons with disabilities are fully integrated as an intimate, integral part of the local body of Christ. God intends his house to be a house of prayer for *all* people (Isaiah 56:7), requiring the elimination of architectural, attitudinal, or theological barriers which prevent people with disabilities from participating and feeling welcomed and valued as part of the fellowship. Hospitality refers to the *posture* we take toward others, not just actions. Seeing people with disabilities as people created in God's image and people whom God loves enables us to assume a reconciled posture of openness and love.

Not much has changed since Badham wrote about the need for open churches and open hearts. Some newer churches address the issue of architectural accessibility, but the more difficult barriers of attitude and theology which prevent, or even dis-invite, people with severe disabilities from participating in worship alongside their nondisabled peers remain, resulting in the continued exclusion of persons who are disabled, which often means the entire family does not participate in the worship service. Reynolds (2008) explained that when a church excludes anyone from its fellowship, the church is diminished because it restricts the redemptive work of God, the essential humanity of those excluded is denied or diminished, and the humanity of those doing the excluding is diminished. Denying someone who is disabled the opportunity to hear the gospel, whether done intentionally or out of ignorance, assuming the person is neither worthy nor capable of receiving God's love, also dishonors *God*, whose love is not limited by a person's disability, no matter how severe. Each human being is created in the image of God, irrespective of ability or achievement; each is a unique person, designed, gifted, and purposed according to God's intent. Failing to reach out and lovingly accept persons affected by disability furthers their isolation and alienation and separates and isolates nondisabled persons. Not respecting and responding to the full range of human ability also limits their own development and perspective on humanity.

Building up others spiritually and relationally starts with love-based reconciliation and includes giving nondisabled and disabled brothers and sisters in Christ opportunities to use their God-given spiritual gifts and natural talents (Psalm 139:13–16). Hale (2012) wrote:

> The church is called to proclaim and reveal this inclusive, not exclusive Kingdom in the way it relates and responds to the needs of people with disabilities and to the divine call to be one human family together with all people. Only then shall it be that everyone – despite not being cured – is healed. (p. 102)

As God's workmanship, we have been "created in Christ Jesus for good works, which God prepared beforehand, that we should walk in them" (Ephesians 2:10). Some Christians fail to apply this teaching to themselves, limiting the "we" to church leaders or missionaries. Understanding Paul to be saying "good works which God has prepared for *us* to walk in" makes it more personal. The "us/we" is not limited to people who are nondisabled but applies to all who follow Christ. It is not only nondisabled persons who are capable of doing good works. Good works result from the presence of the Holy Spirit in Christians. Disability is not stronger than the Spirit of God and does not hold us back from doing good works, but resistance (or outright refusal) to do what, or live as God desires hinders many. Folks with a disability may be more ready to do the works God prepared for them (or prepared them for) than people who are nondisabled, whose fear or low self-esteem becomes an obstacle. Asking a person who is disabled to pray, serve, or read scripture honors both them and the God we serve. Sometimes, by their example, persons with a disability can lead nondisabled people into obediently and humbly serving the Lord. Being physically or intellectually disabled cannot prevent God's grace from working in a person. *Living* with disability can itself be a witness to God's presence. "That is why disabilities are afflictions that heal not only the person but also the community, for we cannot love God, whom we have not seen unless we love our disabled brothers and sisters, whom we have seen" (Kinnard, 2019, p. 43).

Grace. Jesus commanded Christians to take the good news to all peoples of the world, not just those that society or culture deems deserving of God's grace. God's grace *is* grace because no one deserves it. Including people with disabilities in our fellowship is a reminder that we are all present at the table not because our strength or good works earned us a seat, but because God graciously has called us to come and receive his love *just as we are* – vulnerable, broken, wounded, disabled. The power of Jesus's parable in Luke 14 is in the reversal of roles: poor or disabled are not outsiders to God's Kingdom. The outsiders are those with so-called "privilege." Jesus's parable reveals the inclusiveness of the Kingdom of God. Can the same be said of our churches and preaching today?

If the Church is to represent the Kingdom of God visibly, it must invite, welcome, and accept "the poor, crippled, blind, and lame" of the world today. This should be done with the same urgency with which the servants in Jesus's parable were sent to bring them to the banquet (Luke 14:21–24). To have a church building that is beautiful in its architecture and interior design is pleasing. But God's desire is for people to see beyond the physical beauty of the structure and recognize the beauty and glory of God himself. The church is not the building; it is the people. People should be able to "see" the beauty of Christ in our face, spirit, and life. And the church should reflect the beauty and diversity of God's creation. Suppose the church ignores or disregards people and families dealing with disability, failing to reach out in love and welcome them into its fellowship. What picture of Jesus do these people receive?

Some might ask whether a person who is profoundly disabled, especially intellectually, can be saved. Not our problem; we do not save anyone. Salvation is not determined by what we know or how completely we understand all that Jesus has done on the cross. Salvation is found in Who we know and Who knows us. It is a serious matter to God how we, as Christ's representatives, respond to people with disabilities, the poor, and the powerless.

People with disabilities, whether acquired or congenital, bear God's image, just as people with conventional bodies and minds. Jesus said we are to preach the gospel to all peoples and to show love and kindness to others without regard to how well or effectively they respond to us. Hauerwas (2004) remarked, "The demand to be normal can be tyrannical unless we understand that the normal condition of our being together is that we are all different" (p. 40). Recognizing our differences enables us all to flourish as different people. In contrast, human (sinful) pride causes people to elevate themselves above people who display a significant weakness or disability. Focus then falls on the impairment rather than the individual, blinding us to their humanity and beauty as people created in God's image.

Embracing and including the people as Jesus did, gives witness to God's immense, unending, and all-inclusive love. Proclaiming the gospel does not necessitate, nor is it limited to, verbal interaction; it can (and should) be *demonstrated*, making it more "audible" than our words. Ministering to the needs of people in the name of Jesus, motivated by love, can be understood and appreciated even by people who are severely physically or cognitively disabled.

Ortlund (2014) wrote, "The test of a gospel-centered church is its doctrine on paper *plus* its culture in practice" (p. 18). Our busy, overly-scheduled lives may lead us to forget that our primary calling is to follow the Lord. Christianity is a way of life, a way of being and relating. How many who consider themselves Christians understand this? How many think being a Christian is simply their personal, private religion? For how many is being a Christian just something for Sunday mornings or an occasional weeknight group Bible study? For how many does being a Christian make a difference in their lives? God expects every Christian to live the gospel message. Regardless of their vocational calling, every disciple of Christ is to share the gospel wherever they are, through verbal testimony, loving actions, and lifestyle witness. How many understand that Christians, disabled or able-bodied, are called to "be" Jesus in the world?

Hillman (2008) described a Christian's call as "the umbrella under which we function as believers" (p. 198). This functional call entails how we relate to our family and our neighbors in Christian love, how we function in the local body of Christ, and how we serve the greater society in stewardship and mission. Everything that brings us into a relationship with others is part of our call as Christians. Nondisabled individuals often have a false sense of autonomy, which leads them away from God's grace and grace-filled living. Bredin (2007) wrote of the importance of being God's agent of grace and allowing others to be agents of grace to us. He argued, "Christians must create and awaken to the possibilities of relating to people with profound [disabilities] since such personal relationships open them to the beauty of divine grace" (p.4).

Paul often sent greetings to specific people in his epistles; a few were mentioned in 1 Corinthians 16:15–18. As Paul concluded the epistle to the Romans, he extended greetings to many, most of whom we know little or nothing about. They are just names to us, but these individuals were important to Paul and, of course, to God. Men and women are listed. Were they all able-bodied? Did any of them have a disability? We do not know. But Paul specifically said that Apelles (Romans 16:10) is approved, or acceptable, in Christ. Might Apelles have had some kind of disability or weakness? Could Paul have said this of Apelles so the Christians in Rome would understand that disability or weakness did not render him ineligible to serve in the church?

There may be many in the church who serve faithfully despite being disabled, and are examples of faithfulness: reaching others with the gospel, teaching, preaching, serving, or encouraging, if not in words, by example. They do these tasks in the strength God gives them, using their spiritual gifts faithfully and perhaps anonymously behind the scenes. I have mentioned several people in this book with whom I have worked, ministering to and with some, and being ministered to by others. God uses "ordinary" people in extraordinary ways to further his kingdom, whether these "ordinary" people are nondisabled or are "ordinary" people who have a disability. Wolfe and Spangler's (2018) words are significant: "God chooses to work through disability to change both hearts and minds. God does this by revealing his power through disability" (p. 59).

Being a disciple means trusting that God is actively involved in our daily lives and living in submission and dependence. From this place of security, "we're invited to live outwardly, finding creative ways to spill hope into the world" (Dahlstrom, p. 15). What does it mean to embody hope? How do we "spill hope" in the lives of others? How do reconciliation, authenticity, vulnerability, and service play out in our lives and our teaching? Dahlstrom's (2011) comment is relevant:

> The good life is never defined by Jesus in terms of either length or comfort. To the contrary, Jesus says that those who seek to save their life will lose it, and those who lose their lives, spilling them out generously in service to others because of love for God and humanity, will find them … fullness isn't defined by Jesus in terms of length but in terms of depth. (pp. 127–128)

Berge (2015) correctly wrote, "Disability ministry is not a program. It's accepting people with disabilities for who they are and recognizing they have the same opportunity to know and serve the Lord as anyone" (p.4). We need to see the person, not the disability, just as Jesus did.

CHALLENGES TO THE CHURCH

Ortlund's (2014) thoughts on how the church portrays the beauty of Christ raises several questions for consideration concerning disability and the church:

- The church is "ground zero for the new kind of *community* Christ is creating in the world today for the display of his glory" (p. 40). Is God's glory displayed if the church excludes from its purview individuals and families with disabilities as integral parts of the church family? Might God's glory be more dramatically shown when they are welcomed and included?

- "God is creating cultures of hope, expectancy, and good cheer in our churches, so that people can see a glimpse of the future and join in" (p. 55). Can this be said of churches that ignore or exclude individuals and families affected by disability?

- "The gospel creates ... not just a new community, but a new *kind* of community" (p. 65). How will fully including people with disabilities in that new community honor God, bless all the community members, and increase the community's witness to the world?

- "The beauty of human relationships in the church is itself an argument for the gospel" (p. 69). Do people, especially those dealing with disability, sense this beauty of relationship? How does the church portray the beauty of Christ, especially if it ignores individuals and families coping with disability?

- "[God] wants us to behave in ways that reveal his heart and who he is" (p. 70). God's heart is clearly "for" the disabled. Does the church reflect this?

- "The whole point of the beatitudes is to tell us how to behave in the household of God ... The household of God must offer a clear and lovely alternative to the madness of this world" (p. 71). Does the church provide such an alternative? Does the family of God behave in a new way, especially regarding individuals and families dealing with disability?

- "A gospel culture requires us not to bank on our own importance or virtues, but to forsake self-assurance and exult together in Christ Jesus" (p. 82). How might the presence of individuals with disabilities as part of the church community help us to rely on, draw from, and rejoice in Christ?
- "The gospel gives us more than a place to stand; it also leads us into a path to follow" (p. 89). Is your church culture aligned with gospel doctrine? Following that path *should* allow the church to reach out and include people and families with disabilities intentionally.
- "[Gospel] doctrine then creates a culture of gracious acceptance for all kinds of believers" (p. 90). *"All kinds"* refers to both nondisabled and disabled believers.

The instruction of Hebrews 13:18 is that we not neglect to do good and to share what we have because such sacrifices are pleasing to God. It is not enough to simply say to an individual or a family dealing with disability, "I love you" or "God loves you." Love is an action verb. It requires that we *do* something to prove our love is genuine. Jesus did something to demonstrate his love: curing people, feeding people, setting people free from bondage, dying for people. Christians cannot miraculously cure disabled or seriously ill people, and we cannot die for their sins. But we can bring healing and a release from emotional and spiritual bondage through establishing a loving relationship with them, welcoming them into the family of God and into our heart.

AFTERWORD

When our daughter was born profoundly deaf, we knew that many things in our life were about to change. One thing we determined from the beginning that was not going to change was that we were going to treat her the same as we did her older hearing brother.

From the very start, the only concession to her deafness was that we did not expect her to hear us. Otherwise, she would not be treated as a "disabled" child. We insisted that everyone else do the same. As a result, nearly fifty years later she has lived bountifully as a deaf Christian woman highly respected in her profession, and a loving wife and mother in a hearing world.

Certainly, she had the advantage of being raised as a "preacher's kid." The church family was mostly an ideal and nurturing environment. Were there bumps along the way (at home, church, school, college, and everywhere else)? Of course, but we smoothed many of them by recognizing our daughter as a person created in the image of God.

When we recognize a person created in the image of God, we place the "person" first. It is right to recognize a disability, but not helpful if we recognize the individual as a "disabled person," rather than a "person with a disability." The difference may seem like only the transposing of the word "person," but it is much more than that. It is recognizing the person first, not the disability.

In his seminal look on the subject of disability through the ministry and message of the Apostle Paul to the church at Corinth, Dr. David Anderson teaches the body of Christ why placing the person before the disability helps to create an atmosphere of understanding as opposed to an atmosphere of misunderstanding for those among us who live with physical or cognitive limitations.

As you read through this book, you will come to realize that a huge field of both loving care and personal evangelism is wide open to any church willing to reach out to their community with a message of welcome and acceptance to an almost entirely untouched group of persons who are perhaps the most underserved members of our communities - persons with a disability.

Within that community are individuals of extraordinary abilities - abilities that can enrich, enlighten and empower the church in ways otherwise impossible. They are there, waiting and willing to share their own unique gifts. Perhaps the greatest of those gifts is that of simply enriching the banquet table of God's amazing family. "And the master said to the servant, 'Go out to the highways and hedges and compel people to come in, that my house may be filled'" (Luke 14:23).

Dennis D. Frey, Th.D., President
Master's International University of Divinity
Evansville, Indiana
the.mdivs.edu

REFERENCES

Alcorn, Randy. (2009). *If God is Good: Faith in the Midst of Suffering and Evil.* Colorado Springs, CO: Multnomah Books.

American Bible Society. *Contemporary English Version.* 1995.

Anderson, David W. (2013). *Reaching Out and Bringing In: Ministry to and with Persons with Disabilities.* Bloomington, IN: WestBow Press.

Badham, Roger A. (1993). The Second Great Commandment, Xenophobia, and the Mentally Handicapped. *Restoration Quarterly* no. 35 (4):234-239

Barnett, Paul. (1988). *The Message of 2 Corinthians: Power in Weakness.* Downers Grove, IL: IVP Academic.

Beates, Michael S. (2012). Disability and the Gospel: How God Uses our Brokenness to Display His grace. Wheaton, IL: Crossway.

Benner, David G. (1998). *Care of Souls: Revisioning Christian Nurture and Counsel.* Grand Rapids, MI: Baker Books.

Berge, Tait. (2015). A Word to Pastors about Disability Ministry. *The Encourager: The Magazine of Elevate Christian Disability Trust* no. 106:4-5.

Boa, Kenneth. (2001). *Conformed to His Image: Biblical and Practical Approaches to Spiritual Formation.* Grand Rapids, MI: Zondervan.

Bredin, Mark. (2007). *True Beauty: Finding Grace in Disabilities.* Cambridge, England: Grove Books, Ltd.

Brodie, Jessica. (Accessed May 7, 2021). What Every Christian Needs to Know about Koinonia. https://www.crosswalk.com/faith/spiritual-life/what-every-Christian-needs-to-know-about-koinonia.html.

Brown, Cordell. (1996/2003). *I am What I am by the Grace of God.* Warsaw, OH: Echoing Hills Village Foundation.

Browne, Elizabeth J. (1997). *The Disabled Disciple: Ministering in a church without barriers.* Ligouri, MO: Ligouri Publications.

Browning, Don S. (1981). Toward a Practical Theology of Care. *Union Seminary Quarterly Review* no. 36 (2/3):159-172.

Carlson, Dwight L. (1994). *Why do Christians Shoot their Wounded? Helping (Not Hurting) those with Emotional Difficulties.* Downers Grove, Il: InterVarsity Press.

Colson, Emily. (2010). *Dancing with Max: A Mother and Son who Broke Free.* Grand Rapids, MI: Zondervan.

Connor, Benjamin T. (2012). *Amplifying our Witness: Giving Voice to Adolescents with Developmental Disabilities.* Grand Rapids, MI: Eerdmans

Cope, (Mike. 2011). *Megan's Secrets: What my Mentally Disabled Daughter Taught me about Life.* Abilene, TX: Leafwood, Publishers.

Courtney, Freddy. (2011). *Hope: God's Offer to all Mankind.* Bloomington, IN: WestBow Press.

Dahlstrom, Richard. (2011). *The Colors of Hope: Becoming People of Mercy, Justice, and Love.* Grand Rapids, MI: Baker Books.

Deuel, David. (2013). God's Story of Disability: The Unfolding Plan from Genesis to Revelation." *Journal of the Christian Institute on Disability* no. 2 (2):81-96.

Deuel, David C. & John, Nathan G. (2019). *Disability in Mission: The Church's Hidden Treasure*. Peabody, MA: Hendrickson Publishers Marketing.

Eiesland, Nancy. (1994). *The Disabled God: Toward a Liberatory Theology of Disability*. Nashville, TN: Abingdon Press.

Eswine, Zack. (2014). *Recovering Eden: The Gospel According to Ecclesiastes*. Phillipsburg, NJ: P&R Publishing.

Frost, Michael. (2000). *Seeing God in the Ordinary*. Peabody, MA: Hendrickson Publishers.

Geisler, Norman. (2002). *Systematic Theology. Vol. 2*. Minneapolis, MN: Bethany House.

Giesbrecht, Penny. (1988). *Where is God when a Child Suffers?* Hannibal, MO: Hannibal Books.

Guthrie, Donald. (1981). *New Testament Theology*. Downers Grove, IL: InterVarsity Press.

Hale, Nancy. (2012). "The Healing of Acceptance." In *Speaking Out: Gifts of Ministering Undeterred by Disabilities*, edited by Robert L. Walker, 95-102. Charleston, SC: CreateSpace.

Hamilton, James M., Jr. (2014). *What is Biblical Theology: A Guide to the Bible's Story, Symbolism, and Patterns*. Wheaton, IL: Crossway.

Hauerwas, Stanley. (2004). Community and diversity: The tyranny of normality. In *Critical Reflections of Stanley Hauerwas' Theology of Disability: Disabling Society, Enabling Theology*, edited by John Swinton, 37-43. Binghamton, NY: Haworth Pastoral Press.

Hillman, George. (2008). Calling and Spiritual Formation. In *Foundations of Spiritual Formation: A Community Approach to Becoming like Christ*, edited by Paul Pettit, 195-216. Grand Rapids, MI: Kregel Publications.

Hoeksema, Thomas B. (2009). The way we think about disability directly affects how we think about our work: A philosophy of practice for the church services division. In G.L.U.E. Training Manual, edited by Kimberly S. Luurtsema & Barbara J. Newman, 37. Grand Rapids, MI: CLC Network.

Hughes, Gerard W. (2008). God of Surprises. 3rd ed. Grand Rapids, MI: Eerdmans.

Hughes, R. Kent. (2006). 2 Corinthians: Power in Weakness. Wheaton, IL: Crossway.

Johnson, Susanne. Christian Spiritual Formation in the Church and Classroom. Nashville, TN: Abingdon Press, 1989.

Kinard, Summer. (2019). Of Such is the Kingdom: A Practical Theology of Disability. Chesterton, IN: Ancient Faith Publishing.

Kovac, Sarah. (2013). In Capable Arms: Living a Life Embraced by Grace. Nashville, TN: Abingdon Press.

Langer, Rick. (2011). Disability, Calling, and 'a Kind of Life Imposed on Man.' In Beyond Suffering: A Christian View on Disability Ministry, edited by Joni Eareckson Tada & Steve Bundy, Course Reader CD-ROM, Reading #15. Agoura Hills, CA: The Christian Institute of Disability, Joni and Friends International Disability Center.

Lawrence, Michael. (2010). Biblical Theology in the Life of the Church. Wheaton, IL: Crossway.

Longchar, W. Wati. (2011). Sin, Suffering, and Disability in God's World. In Disability, Society, and Theology: Voices from Africa, edited by Samuel Kabue, Ester Mombo, Joseph Galgala, & C. B. Peter, 47-58. Limuru, Kenya: Zapf Chancery Publishers Africa, Ltd.

MacArthur, John. (2003). 2nd Corinthians: The MacArthur New Testament Commentary. Chicago, IL: Moody Press.

McCloughry, Roy, & Morris, Wayne. (2002). *Making a World of Difference.* London: Society for Promoting Christian Knowledge (SPCK).

McIntosh, Jen. (2017). *Beautifully Broken: A Journey through the Bible for Parents of Children with Special Needs.* Bloomington, IN: WestBow Press.

McNair, Jeff. "The Power of Those Who Seem Weaker: People with Disabilities in the Church." *Journal of the Christian Institute on Disability 3*, no. 1 (2014): 143-57

McNair, Jeff. *The Church and Disability 2: The Weblog Disabled Christianity.* CreateSpace Independent Publishing Platform, 2016.

Meininger, Herman P. "Authenticity in Community: Theory and Practice of an Inclusive Anthropology in Care for Persons with Intellectual Disabilities." In *Spirituality and Intellectual Disability: International Perspectives of the Effect of Culture and Religion on Healing Body, Mind, and Soul*, edited by William C. Gaventa & David L. Coulter. 13-28. New York: The Haworth Press, 2001..

Merrill, Eugene H. *Everlasting Dominion: The Story of the Old Testament.* Nashville, TN: B&H Publishing, 2020.

Millar, Gary. *2 Corinthians for You.* Charlotte, NC: The Good Book Company, 2020.

Morstad, David. *Whole Community: Introducing Communities of Faith to People with Intellectual and Developmental Disabilities.* Bloomington, IN: WestBow Press, 2018.

Mouw, Richard J. *Uncommon Decency: A Christian Civility in an Uncivil World.* Downers Grove, IL: InterVarsity Press, 1992.

Nicole, Roger. *Standing Forth: Collected Writings of Roger Nicole.* Great Britain: Christian Focus Publications, 2002.

Nouwen, Henri J. M. *Reaching Out: Three Movements of the Spiritual Life.* New York: Image Books/Doubleday, 1975.

Nouwen, Henri J. M. *Adam: God's Beloved.* Maryknoll, NY: Orbis Books, 1997..

Ortlund, Ray. *The Gospel: How the Church Portrays the Beauty of Christ.* Wheaton, IL: Crossway, 2014.

Parrett, Gary. A. & Kang, S. Steve. *Teaching the Faith, Forming the Faithful: A Biblical Vision for Education in the Church.* Downers Grove, IL: IVP Academic, 2009

Petersen, Jim. *Lifestyle Discipleship: The Challenge of Jesus in Today's World.* Colorado Springs, CO: NavPress, 1993.

Peterson, Eugene H. *The Message: The Bible in Contemporary English.* Colorado Springs, CO: NavPress, 2002.

Phillips, John B. *Your God Is Too Small.* New York: Touchstone (Simon and Schuster), 2004. Original edition, 1952.

Piper, John. "But by the Grace of God: 2 Corinthians 12:9." In, *Solid Joys Devotional* no. January 1, 2021 (2021).

Pohl, Christine D. "Hospitality from the Edge: The Significance of Marginality in the Practice of Welcome." *The Annual of the Society of Christian Ethics* (1995): 121-136.Pohl, Christine D. (2003). Biblical Issues in Mission and Migration. *Missiology: An International Review* no. 31 (1):1-15.

Pohl, Cristine D. *Living in Community: Cultivating Practices That Sustain Us.* Grand Rapids, MI: Eerdmans, 2012.

Prior, David. *The Message of 1 Corinthians: Life in the Local Church.* Downers Grove, IL: InterVarsity Press, 1985.

Reimer, Justin. "Deciding to Go on Mission with Disability." In *Disability in Mission: The Church's Hidden Treasure*, edited by David C.Deuel & Nathan G. John. 121-32. Peabody, MA: Hendrikson Publishers Marketing, 2019.

Reinders, Hans S. *Receiving the Gift of Friendship: Profound Disability, Theological Anthropology, and Ethics*. Grand Rapids, MI: Eerdmans, 2008.

Reynolds, Thomas E. "Welcoming without Reserve? A Case in Christian Hospitality." *Theology Today 6*, no. 3 (2006): 191-202.

Reynolds, Thomas E. *Vulnerable Communion: A Theology of Disability and Hospitality*. Grand Rapids, MI: Brazos Press, 2008.

Rivera, Ted. *Reforming Mercy Ministry: A Practical Guide to Loving your Neighbor*. Downers Grove, IL: InterVarsity Press, 2014.

Ryle, John Charles. *Holiness: It's Nature, Hindrances, Difficulties, and Roots*. Reprint (originally published 1879) ed. Grand Rapids, MI: Kregel Publications, 1956.

Scazzero, Peter. *Emotionally Healthy Spirituality: It's Impossible to Be Spiritually Mature, While Remaining Emotionally Immature*. Updated ed. Grand Rapids, MI: Zondervan, 2017

Shelp, Earl E. "Caregiving as Sustaining Presence." *Church and Society 93*, no. 5 (2003): 31-35.

Shults, F. LeRon & Sandage, Steven J. *Transforming Spirituality: Integrating Theology and Psychology*. Grand Rapids, MI: Baker Academic, 2006..

Smart, Julie. *Disability, Society, and the Individual*. Austin, TX: Pro-Ed, 2001.

Stott, John. *The Contemporary Christian: Applying God's Word to Today's World*. Downers Grove, IL: InterVarsity Press, 1992.

Swinton, John. "From Inclusion to Belonging: A Practical Theology of Community, Disability, and Humanness." *Journal of Religion, Disability, & Health 16*, no. 2 (2012): 175-90.

Tada, Joni Eareckson. *A Lifetime of Wisdom: Embracing the Way God Heals You*. Grand Rapids, MI: Zondervan, 2009.

Tada, Joni Eareckson & Estes, Steven. *A Step Further: Growing Closer to God through Hurt and Hardship*. Grand Rapids, MI: Zondervan, 1976/2001.

Tada, Joni Eareckson & Estes, Steven. *A Step Further: Growing Closer to God through Hurt and Hardship*. Grand Rapids, MI: Zondervan, 1976/2001.

Tiffany, Frederick C. & Ringe, Sharon H. *Biblical Interpretation: A Roadmap*. Nashville, TN: Abingdon Press. 1996.

Tozer, Aiden Wilson. "May 8 Entry." In *Evenings with Tozer: Daily Devotional Readings*, edited by compiled by Gerald B. Smith. Chicago, IL: Moody Publishers, 1981.

Vanier, Jean. *From Brokenness to Community*. Mahwah, NJ: Paulist Press, 1992.

Venzke, Katie E. (2018). A Christ-Reflecting Church: Philosophy of Ministry. *Journal of the Christian Institute on Disability 7*, no. 1 Spring/Summer (2918): 25-47.

Walker, Robert L. *Speaking Out: Gifts of Ministering Undeterred by Disabilities*. Charleston, SC: CreateSpace, 2012.

Webb-Mitchell, Brett. *Unexpected Guests at God's Banquet: Welcoming People with Disabilities into the Church*. New York: The Crossroad Publishing Co., 1994.

Webb-Mitchell, Brett. *Dancing with Disabilities: Opening the Church to all God's Children*. Eugene, OR: Wipf & Stock., 2008.

Webb-Mitchell, Brett. *Beyond Accessibility: Toward Full Inclusion of People with Disabilities in Faith Communities*. New York: Church Publishing, 2010.

Wilson, Geoffrey B. *1 Corinthians: A Digest of Reformed Comment*. London: Banner of Truth Trust, 1971.

Wolfe, Ryan & Spangler, Gary. *My Friends, My Teachers: Life Changing Encounters with Disability*. Louisville, TN: Ability Ministry, 2018.

Wright, Nicholas Thomas. *Paul for Everyone: 2 Corinthians*. Louisville, KY: Westminster John Knox Press, 2004.

Yong, Amos. *The Bible, Disability, and the Church: A New Vision of the People of God*. Grand Rapids, MI: Eerdmans, 2011.

HELPFUL WEBSITE RESOURCES

Joni and Friends International Disability Center:
www.joniandfriends.org

Irresistible Church Training Series for Special Needs:
www.joniandfreinds.org/ministries/church-training-resources/
irresistible-church-training-series

Canyon Hills Community Church-Special Needs Ministry:
www.canyonhillscommunitychurch.com

Bridge Ministries:
www.bridgeministries.org

Tim Tebow "Night to Shine"
www.timtebowfoundation.org

Echoing Hills Village:
www.echoinghills.org

Young Life Capernaum:
https://capernaum.younglife.org

Friendship Ministries:
https://friendship.org

DisAbility Ministry:
www.abilityministry.com

Crossing Bridges, Inc.
www.crossingbridgesinc.org

Printed in the United States
by Baker & Taylor Publisher Services